RICCARDO MUTI: AN AUTOBIOGRAPHY

Riccardo Muti

an autobiography

FIRST THE MUSIC, THEN THE WORDS

EDITED BY MARCO GRONDONA

TRANSLATED FROM THE ITALIAN BY ALTA L. PRICE

RIZZOLI
NEW YORK

New York · Paris · London · Milan

75571647

First published in English in the United States of America in 2011 by
RIZZOLI EX LIBRIS, a division of Rizzoli International Publications, Inc.
300 Park Avenue South
New York, NY 10010
www.rizzoliusa.com

First published in Italian under the title *Prima la musica, poi le parole* in 2010 by
RCS Libri S.p.A., Milano.

2011 2012 2013 2014 / 10 9 8 7 6 5 4 3 2 1

TRANSLATED FROM THE ITALIAN BY Alta L. Price
DESIGNED BY Sara E. Stemen

PRINTED IN THE UNITED STATES OF AMERICA

ISBN-13: 978-0-8478-3724-3
LIBRARY OF CONGRESS CATALOGUE CONTROL NUMBER: 2011931513

PHOTO INSERT CREDITS
All photographs © Silvia Lelli by courtesy of www.riccardomuti.com,
with the exception of the following:
pp. 11, 14, 16 © Graziella Vigo
pp. 20, 22 (top) © Jean E. Brubaker
p. 21 (bottom) © Lelli and Masotti
p. 29 © Steve J. Sherman

The publisher has made every effort to obtain permission from
the respective copyright owners, and welcomes any inadvertently
omitted copyright owners to contact them for proper credit.

E come giga e arpa, in tempra tesa
di molte corde, fa dolce tintinno
a tal da cui la nota non è intesa,
così da' lumi che lì m'apparinno
s'accogliea per la croce una melode
che mi rapiva, sanʒa intender l'inno.

And as a lute and harp, accordant strung
with many strings, a dulcet tinkling make
to him by whom the notes are not distinguished,

so from the lights that there to me appeared
upgathered through the cross a melody,
which rapt me, not distinguishing the hymn.

DANTE ALIGHIERI, *Paradiso*, XIV: 118–123
(TRANS. HENRY WADSWORTH LONGFELLOW)

Contents

Translator's Note *Alta L. Price*

TRANSLATION is a great honor, pleasure, challenge, and responsibility. I have endeavored to bring Maestro Muti's life story to English-language readers in the most direct way possible. Those familiar with opera will already know that the Italian language possesses a musicality that is invariably lost in any other language. The translator Ralph Manheim once observed that translators are much like actors, speaking the author's lines as the author himself would if he could speak English. Considered from a musical standpoint, the translator is to the author as the musician is to the composer: the ultimate goal is a superb interpretation of the text/score.

Bearing this in mind, I would like to clarify a few key details. First and foremost, Muti uses the term "melodrama" throughout the book, and I have preserved this use of it, resisting the temptation to render it simply as "opera" or "lyric opera" or "operatic arts." As the *Oxford English Dictionary* notes, this hybrid term—from the Greek *melos*, "song, music," and French *drame*, "drama"—historically referred to a "play with songs interspersed and orchestral music accompanying the action." Although it has since acquired the often derogatory connotation of an overly sensational type of drama, it is, as Muti states in chapter 7, in this more accurate, historical sense that he uses the word.

Titles of orchestral or operatic works and specific arias are a slippery subject: sometimes they have a standard, widely known translation (*Le nozze di Figaro* as *The Marriage of Figaro*); often they do not (*Così fan tutte*). I have used the standard English titles where applicable, and all other works appear with their original titles, occasionally adding clarification where necessary (*La Traviata*). Nonoperatic works with standard titles translated over various languages—such as the piece Muti refers to as *Chiaro di luna*, which English speakers would more readily recognize as the *Moonlight* Sonata, German speakers would know as *die Mondscheinsonate*, and French speakers would call *Claire de lune*—also appear in English. Because most famous arias are known by a line or two of the original lyrics ("Va', pensiero"), I have kept the original Italian and provided an English translation where comprehension of Muti's reflections depends on a clear understanding of what is being sung.

Author's Note

I have taken for my book the famous title of Giovanni Battista Casti's libretto for the opera *Prima la musica e poi le parole* by Antonio Salieri. Those who know me might find this contradictory, and those who read just a few more pages into this book—especially with regard to the performances of *Così fan tutte* in Salzburg—will discover that I always like to begin with the "words," for in theater I expect them to be perfectly distinct, above and beyond the music. Here, however, I just wanted to explain the need I feel—at age seventy, after fifty years in music—to pause and reflect upon my life and myself, and turn my reflections into *words*.

CHAPTER ONE

A Violin Instead of a Toy

*A*ndiam. *Incominciate!* As Tonio commands at the beginning of *Pagliacci*, "Let's go, begin!" Like a lot of other music, the tranquil and metaphysical voice of that prelude has accompanied me throughout my life.

Let's begin, then, by clarifying where I was born, because there's always confusion about that. Some claim I'm Apulian, others claim I'm Neapolitan, and somehow the citizens of Molfetta seem to resent the fact that—for objective reasons—I cannot *not* say that I was born in Naples. It happened on July 28, 1941, during the war. My mother was as Neapolitan as they come, and my father was Apulian. I was born in Naples, but they brought me straight back to Molfetta, and I harbor the same love for both hometowns: I like to call myself an Apulo-Campanian.

I was born in Naples, despite the fact that my father Domenico was a doctor in Apulia, because my mother, Gilda Peli-Sellitto, was incredibly proud of her native city. Each time one of us five children was about to be born, she would take the train, return to Naples, have the baby, and only a few days later bring us back to Molfetta. From the time we reached the age of discretion, we all thought it an odd decision. Why, we asked her, did she embark on a trip that—at least in my case, since it was the second year of the war—was long, tiring, and even dangerous? She replied, not knowing that at least one of us would lead a globetrotting life primarily outside of Italy, with a phrase that didn't strike us at the time but now I can't help but see as prophetic: "If, one day, you travel the world and end up—who knows?—in America, when they ask you where you were born and you reply, 'In Naples,' they'll respect you." She pronounced the verb *rispettare* adding a *c* to the *s* as only Neapolitans do, so it sounded like "reshpect." "But if you were to say, 'In Molfetta,' you'd have to waste a bit of time explaining where it is."

She said this, of course, without any offense whatsoever to the people of Molfetta. It's a great place that has also given birth to illustrious figures: not only the learned abbot Vito Fornari and the great painter Corrado Giaquinto but, more recently, Gaetano Salvemini[1] (who was married to a cousin of my father's, and who occasionally came up in family conversation).

They brought me to Molfetta when I was fourteen days old, and I lived there for sixteen years. I began my studies at a school named after Alessandro Manzoni, and in my last three years there my grandfather Donato Muti was my teacher. He was the principal as well. He taught with a strictness that, throughout my formative years from adolescence to early adulthood, ended up being extremely important. In both middle and high school (I went to the same institute where Salvemini had been a student) the teachers' strictness was a constant. Even in middle school they addressed us by the formal "you," *lei*, so that to this day I have a hard time addressing people by the informal *tu*; it's a question of upbringing and manners. When I was little, the constant use of the formal *lei* made a real impression on

me—especially in certain circumstances, such as an in-class reprimand. In that case the relationship between teacher and pupil
fell into the oxymoronic situation where you could no longer tell
if it was being used out of scorn or respect. More than once I
heard teachers use the formal *lei* when shouting reprimands like
"You are a dummy!"

I recall, for example, that in Latin class one day during the
first year of middle school, Mr. Delzotti grabbed me by my ear
and hauled me up, inflicting real pain. It was all because of his
ominous "pluit aqua": he asked me what case it was and I, who
obviously hadn't done the homework, replied "Nominative."
He dragged me up to his desk, continuously badgering me,
with a degree of relish: "Nominative, eh? Nominative, eh?
Nominative, eh?" Another time, when I had to translate "mus
est farinam" (the mouse eats the flour)—with that "est" that's
as insidious as the heart corroded by passion in Horace's epistle
("si quid est animum")[2]—I confused "to eat" (*edo, es, est . . .*)
and "to be," and he railed at me with that same inexorable rigor.
These are things that now make me reflect on the sheer strange-
ness of those teachers, so different from today's, and even from
the ones my children had. I don't know what went on elsewhere,
but in southern Italy right after the end of the war, disciplinary
practices were so ironclad and teaching methods so harsh that
now they'd lead straight to the teacher's arrest.

That's not the way I operate, but I have to say that such
methods didn't provoke any particular psychological complex;
rather, they allow me, for example, to still deploy a fairly pass-
able Latin—something that often attracts curiosity abroad.
So the feeling I have for all my teachers is one of gratitude.

Ultimately, they were just asking for a bit of proper behavior; they expected us to be "adults" rather than adolescents.

One morning one of my Italian teachers, Angelo Tangari, was teaching a literature class and heard someone make a noise. He asked who had done it, and no one replied, so he threatened to punish the entire class, whereupon someone said: "It was he!" Tangari gestured at the culprit, who admitted his guilt and was expelled that same morning. After the bell rang at one o'clock, the teacher stood near the door as usual while each student said goodbye on the way out. When the tattletale walked up, the teacher kept him in the classroom and closed the door, and no one knows what he said. An episode of this sort will remind many readers familiar with Italian literature of a scene in Edmondo De Amicis's 1886 classic *Cuore*: "The teacher, quite pale, went to his table and, in an irritated voice, asked: 'Who did it?'"[3]

Seventy years had passed since the first edition of De Amicis's novel was published, but the climate was the same: strictness at home and strictness in school. I don't want to say what's right or wrong. I'm just telling you about the environment I grew up in, and by so doing I also hope to justify a certain reserve I have. It's often viewed as intentional aloofness or, worse, haughtiness or arrogance. That's not how I am. I'm convinced that there's even a degree of timidity beneath it all. (I might sometimes seem "austere" or "severe," but one night in Milan in more recent years I ran into Gigi Proietti[4] and Roberto Benigni at the corner of Via Manzoni and Via Montenapoleone and we cracked a few jokes; they were surprised I knew so many amusing anecdotes.)

My father was an excellent doctor, and was born with the qualities that add up to the so-called clinical eye: few tools but a vast knowledge of diagnostics. People in Molfetta still remember "dottor Muti," especially the older folks whose children he treated. He was almost always working, and after making the rounds of his patients (who were known then as *mutuati*⁵) he regularly dedicated some of his time to religious communities. There were many in town, starting with the regional pontifical seminary and the episcopal seminary, which taught children up until high school. So throughout my childhood I was often found skipping through the corridors of convents and monasteries.

I was quite comfortable in such environments, and one day when I was little, I caused a slight scandal in the basilica of Santa Maria dei Martiri. This very old Capuchin church had a hospital annex built during the Crusades, with a gigantic ward where we went for lunch once every year. (I can still see the monks' long white beards and fire-filled eyes, details straight out of Melitone's story in *La forza del destino*.) While the monks celebrated Mass, I climbed up to the console of the organ and, for Communion, dared to play the "Brindisi" from *La Traviata*. Frequenting those places and the monks and nuns (whom I sometimes helped peel potatoes or feed acorns to the pigs) brought me into contact with a world that already belonged to the distant past, places that now seem like nineteenth-century realms. This must also have influenced me, not in any confessional sense—on the contrary, it gave me a critical stance toward any and all fundamentalism-tinged close-mindedness—but rather in the sense of an entirely particular culture that, in that place and time, was very much alive. You mustn't forget that, in those years, television's presence was so spotty as to be virtually nonexistent.

I remember that back then in Molfetta, which wasn't such a small town, two things were incredibly rare: telephones and cars. I first saw a telephone at my friend Pansini's house, and felt both awe and envy. Toward the end of the forties my dad got around town in a horse-drawn cart driven by a coachman. Nicola, the coachman, always bragged about having been a soldier in the assault troops during World War I, and still kept his infantry dagger closely guarded. One day when I was in Florence a friend loaned me a book, Renato Fucini's *Le veglie di Neri*, which had become popular there because of its focus on the Tuscan countryside. There's a chapter about Fucini's father, a municipal district doctor who one snowy day, as he took off on a horse to make his rounds, scolded his son in the most menacing tones: "Remember how your father earns his money."[6] Well, things weren't so different in postwar Molfetta. But when we all traveled together, for festivals in the nearby towns of Andria, Terlizzi, Bisceglie, or Giovinazzo, we went by carriage. One evening we left town by carriage in order to get to Castel del Monte by dawn; opening the curtains, I was surprised to find the castle built by Holy Roman Emperor Frederick II right before my eyes, like an enormous crown fallen from heaven, a striking sight I've never forgotten.

In 1950 the horse was replaced by a car when my parents bought a Fiat Giardinetta. It was mostly for my father's work, but in the summers we'd sometimes use it to go to Naples, where we'd spend a few vacation days with my maternal grandmother. The driver and my mother sat up front, my father and my two older brothers squeezed into the backseat, and they set up a wooden bench in the trunk for me and the twins. All told, between my parents and the driver and us kids, there were eight of us, and the towering mound of baggage strapped to the roof was a sight you'd now see only in some neorealist film. There was no highway, so we drove on regional and provincial roads for almost ten hours, and the car had a hard time on hills. After Bovino and Ariano Irpino the road ascended to Dentecane, and Dad urged the driver to rev up, shouting "Scèmme, Lui', scèmme!"[7]

When we teenagers spent our afternoons hanging out around the so-called Villa Comunale—it was our main street of sorts, not a bona fide villa but more like a circular park close to the sea where everyone in Molfetta went for a stroll—we'd run into our teachers and talk about philosophy and all our problems. We were like young Peripatetics, yet also young flaneurs trying to flirt with girls for the first time. The absolute height of excitement was when the girls, walking in the opposite direction, passed and looked at us for two seconds. You couldn't imagine a more sublime love: we went out solely to get a glance!

All this happened in front of the large clock on the episcopal seminary, decorated with the delightful inscription "Mortales vos esse docet quae labitur hora," one of those humanistic hexameters I later found in various alternate versions during my travels around Italy. They all had the essential concept of *labitur* in common—"Mortals, this passing hour says you, too, will pass!"; one time I saw an inscription that read "Fallimur imperiis it gloria labitur aetas."[8] What a fundamental contrast, love being born below such a clock. When I became a "grown-up" and began conducting *Don Giovanni*, I thought of that every time I came to the scene where the libertine takes his watch from his pocket. (I also found echoes of that inscription emanating from the heap of watches on the set of Luca Ronconi's 1999 production of *Don Giovanni* in Salzburg.) This particular perception of death is much more present in southern Italy, where it's as if Libitina[9] keeps her finger pointed at such memento mori from dawn to dusk. Just think, when I was a kid our town still had *prefiche*, women that by now only a few Italians might remember from the pages of *Morte e pianto rituale* (Death and Ritual Mourning).[10] When someone passed away, these women would go to the deceased's home and recite, for pay, a *laudatio funebris*—to be precise, the one described in De Martino's book as Ferrandina's lament: "O Ciccille mie, o belle, o frate, o frate, o Ciccille mie."[11] Perhaps the last and most famous *prefica* was one Giustina "del Camposanto" (Justine "of the Cemetery"): I can still picture her, always dressed entirely in black—a predominant color in those days, particularly in Molfetta.

*

My father had an exquisite tenor voice, and I regularly heard him singing arias by Mascagni and Leoncavallo. My grandfather, Donato the strict schoolmaster, who didn't have much of a voice, had a habit of singing, too: he often sang arias from *Norma*, and once I even heard him sing a few notes of *Attila*. There was actually an immense love of opera in my family—as there was across many different levels of society at the time—and it was greatly nurtured by local bands whose operatic *fantasias* brought music to the people. Virtually no one had records, and many people didn't even own a radio.

The first time my parents took me to the Teatro Petruzzelli in Bari, I was three. I sat on the coachman's lap and listened to

Aida without crying or causing the slightest disturbance—or so they told me.

Soon thereafter my father decided all his children should study music in one form or another. He saw it as a fundamental part of a good upbringing, without which you couldn't become a well-rounded person. My older brothers took up the guitar and the accordion—instruments they chose of their own volition, I think. I didn't give it the slightest thought; I wasn't interested, so I hadn't chosen anything. In Molfetta we celebrated Saint Nick's Day, or Santa Nicola as we called him in dialect, on December 6, the day most children received presents—the equivalent of Christmas or Epiphany for children elsewhere in Italy and abroad. All I got, on that long-ago morning in 1948, was a small case with a three-quarter violin. I was so disappointed that it wasn't a toy. Yet there it was, before my eyes, a sign that something terrible awaited me, that something awful was about to begin. Indeed, soon thereafter they introduced me to my solfeggio teacher, who walked me through the scale. I can picture her to this day: she was a young blonde. Nevertheless, my hatred of solfeggio remained strong enough that I made no progress in the first three months. My brain balked at the very idea and refused to learn a thing. She would point to a line on the staff, and I'd just make whatever sound came first, as I didn't recognize a single note. In the end, she asked my father to just let it go.

She'd convinced him and, albeit reluctantly, he was ready to give up; the family would have one nonmusical child, so be it. My mother, on the other hand—to my great surprise, because she didn't have any particular interest in music—made a strange remark: "Let's give it another month." Most family-related decisions—the ones we called "irrevocable"—were up to her. I don't know why she said that, nor exactly what switch it flipped within me, but everything became clear to me that night. The following morning, in front of my teacher, I recognized all the notes quickly and with a degree of boldness, even. So I was finally able to move on from solfeggio to really begin playing the violin.

My first teacher was Aldo Gigante, who started by showing me the positions of the left hand on the fingerboard, bow handling, and so on—the rudimentary basics. It was hard at first. I tried playing the open strings as I stood in front of a window in our house that looked onto Piazza Paradiso and saw my peers out playing soccer; from that point of view it was difficult not to hate the violin, and my progress once again slowed to a crawl. Then at one point, I don't remember how, I again experienced a sudden shift and made a leap forward—so much so that in 1950, with Gigante accompanying me on the piano, I played Vivaldi's Concerto in A Major before an audience of three hundred pontifical seminarians. The concert, which was written up in the *Gazzetta del Mezzogiorno* newspaper, was an evening event where a small orchestra and the seminary chorus performed a few pieces after mine. (One of the seminarians was Tonino Bello, who became a well-known bishop in Molfetta, and the rector was Corrado Ursi, who later became cardinal and archbishop of Naples.)

But I also need to mention something that happened a few years before. When I began studying the violin in Molfetta, I had a unique experience. As a highly respected doctor, my father often did rounds, as I mentioned, at seminaries, convents, and parishes. One of them invited me to deliver a Christmas sermon for the Chiesa dell'Immacolata, right near our house. So for two months I took acting lessons from a poor, churchy seamstress—a sexton of sorts. She sewed little more than pants for local farmers, not really anything that would have been called tailoring, but she showed me the gestures to use as I spoke in order to win the congregation's esteem. I had to start out with "Christus natus est nobis, venite, adoremus," turn to the right as I added "reverendissimo parroco," and then address the whole audience as I said "signori." I no longer remember a single word of it. I had to go to the episcopal seminary to get outfitted, and I tried on various seminarians' habits until I found one that fit; it had red buttons (the habits of the pontifical seminary had black buttons). They handed me the parish priest's large tricorne and a surplice. The evening of the sermon, all my relatives packed into the crowded church, and when I went to greet the parish priest at the end, my grandfather gave me 500 lire. That was an enormous sum back then, especially for my grandfather, who, because he had experienced both wealth and poverty, was quite cautious when it came to spending anything. It's amusing to think that I, who never even considered becoming a seminarian, once wore a frock for two hours!

When I was little, going with my father on his rounds and running around the halls of the pontifical seminary, there weren't many sources of amusement, so even exploring the large science lecture hall, for example, could be considered a worthy pastime. Because I had just enrolled at the conservatory in Bari, the seminarians decided to include me in their annual theatrical performance. The show was open to the public and to countless relatives. People came from all over Apulia, Calabria, and Basilicata. I was to direct *Raggio di sole* (Ray of Sun), a little opera in which my twin siblings acted alongside other seminarians. There was a chorus—the part I remember most—in which the seminarians, wearing the knickerbockers so fashionable at the time, sang lines no less improbable than "Veniam dai grattacieli di New York, passammo tutto a piedi il Canadà" (We're from the skyscrapers of New York, we crossed Canada on foot). I thought it strange that they were dressed so differently than they usually were. When I saw them on the streets of Molfetta they had round broad-brimmed hats, wore little capes, and walked in pairs in a line ("As go the Minor Friars along their way");[12] they were as different from my knickerbockered chorus as day is from night. I was quite strict with them, despite the relatively lightweight opera.

I was equally strict at Christmas when I directed "La santa allegrezza" (The Holy Joy), a traditional Christmastime carol in Molfetta. Back in the day, as my father told it, this piece was sometimes performed solo or by impromptu carolers who'd come up to the doors of lower-class locals—of whom there were still a lot. The lyrics went: "Cantare io voglio / la santa allegrezza, / di Dio bellezza, / a maggior dignità. / S'è incarnato in la Vergine pia / lasciando a Maria la verginità / con amor tanto, con amor tanto: / così volle lo Spirito Santo."[13] Then the temporary troubadors requested a few coins in exchange for their performance.

It must have been 1956, and people had decided to have group competitions, since the Christmastime carolers had by then become tradition, and the "Allegrezza" was often sung by a small chorus, accompanied by a guitar, a violin, an accordion, a double bass, and other instruments, going from door to door and sharing, as the title promised, "the holy joy." After a few stanzas the hostess would offer her callers some sweets and dessert liqueurs like rosolio, and it had soon become customary for the carolers to end the long song with the request (in dialect) "Uè la patrona, uè la patrona, issa o canistru e da' cosa bona" (Hey hostess, hey hostess, hoist up the basket and give us some goodies). So we participated in the competition, and I, along with my group, won. I played the violin and led an ensemble that included a guitar, an accordion, a mandolin, and a three-string double bass. The bass was enormous. I had found it in the ground-floor barbershop right near my house, and since these songs were always composed with tonic, dominant, and subdominant notes, without even a submediant, I'd tuned it to B-flat, E-flat, and F; we played the concluding bit, begging for refreshments, in B-flat. The prize was a cup I've hung on to all these years, my first musical heirloom. I was directing people older than I was, but even though my future profession wasn't so much as a twinkle in my eye yet, I was quite exigent and demanded precise pitch. The poor guy who played the three-string double bass had his work cut out for him—he had to know exactly when to play the E-flat, the F, and the B-flat! I required such rigorous rehearsals that they mounted a mutiny one day: they were late for practice because they'd stopped on the way to plan a revolt on my front doorstep. Thinking back on it now, I smile, but evidently I was convinced that that music—simple as it may have been—had to be blessed with the utmost precision and played with absolute moral devotion. And in the end, all the "musicians" were quite happy.

During those same months the seminarians who'd performed *Raggio di sole* commissioned me to compose a four-part choral piece for them to sing on the occasion of their consecration to the priesthood. Again, I wasn't giving the slightest thought to what I'd do in the future, but I look back on these events as unique harbingers along life's path. I wrote my a cappella piece, *Tu es sacerdos in aeternum*, in a counterpoint that strikes me now as fairly uncertain, but at the time I really liked it. The seminarians must have found it overly complicated, though, because they never sang it. Like the cup, I have hung on to the sheet music for this composition.

I started out as a violinist and continued studying that instrument for several more years, until my teacher suggested how essential a background in piano was. For the first few years I studied piano with Ms. De Judicibus, whose teacher had in turn studied with Florestano Rossomandi, an important leader of the Neapolitan school. I fell in love with the instrument: whereas the violin forced me to find a partner, with the piano I could play both the melody and the accompaniment, and that seemed to me a real miracle. I was soon ready for the fifth-year exam.

All this took place while I continued my regular course of study in school. Despite his deep faith in music, my father didn't envision me becoming a professional musician. Rather, as was common in small towns back then, he thought of music and the musical world as something distant and even slightly alien. At most he might imagine me becoming a teacher and conductor of the local band. So I abandoned the violin in favor of the piano and enrolled at the Piccinni Conservatory in Bari—but I'm getting ahead of myself, and I'd rather go chronologically.

It was 1955 and my exam program included, among other works, Chopin's Polonaise no. 4 in G-sharp minor. I got there in the morning and waited my turn. Hours passed. By two o'clock it was late, it was hot, we were hungry, and our fears were mounting. The exam committee wore black bow ties like musicians used to once upon a time, as did Maestro Pasquale La Rotella; you can only imagine what an impression it all made on me, a boy who'd grown up in the fantastical world of Good Fridays, "Povera Rosa,"[14] and the traditional funeral marches of Molfetta! All of a sudden there appeared at the door a small man with radiant, penetrating eyes. He asked how many of us were left: three. I ventured a question, perhaps out of fear: "Can we come back tomorrow?" He stared at me and then took me to another room, told me to play something for him, and assured me in no uncertain terms, "You'll take the exam today." After my rehearsal the small man stood up and said to me, in front of everyone, "We're giving you an A+. Not for how you played today, but for how you could in the future." That man's name was Nino Rota. He was the conservatory director, and he traveled back and forth between Bari and Rome, so he was often absent, but as fate would have it, that day he was there, and he spoke to me. I went home triumphant and thought no more would come of it.

That September my father had to go to the INAM (Istituto nazionale dell'assistenza sanitaria, the National Health Service of the time) in Bari for a file, and I went along. We were driven by Peppino, a chauffeur I later encountered again in America, after he'd emigrated to Hoboken, New Jersey. While my father tended to business, I went with Peppino to check the grades posted on a landing at the music institute. I was overjoyed at the sight of my string of A+ grades. While we were there, someone walked past behind me, turned, and asked: "You're Mutino, aren't you?" (He used the diminutive of my last name. Even today I'm not all that tall, but when I was younger I grew so slowly my mother sometimes complained, "Chisto ccà nun cresce maie, stu guaglione," dialect for "This one here'll never grow, this boy.") It was, once again, Maestro Rota, who took me to his office and advised me to enroll, because I had talent and should therefore be among other music students. That meant moving a long way: Molfetta is about twenty miles from Bari, but none of us had ever left home. We held a major family meeting and decided we'd need to speak with the director. So we all went to see Rota, and in the end it was concluded I was to study with Franco Ruggero, a magnificent maestro of the Neapolitan school. (Vitale writes about him at length in his superb book.)[15]

It was 1956. Each morning I went to first-year classes at the *liceo classico*,[16] and each afternoon I took a bus that crawled along State Route 16 at a snail's pace, passing through Giovinazzo, Santo Spirito, and Palese, and eventually got to Bari. As is usually the case, I'd imagine, my high school teachers didn't care in the least that I was taking music lessons as well (and vice versa: neither institution accepted any excuses), so I had to be a good student on both fronts. Rota always closely supported me with real affection, advice, and attention. Under his tutelage I heard my first quartet and saw my first real concert when he directed the Bari orchestra and chorus. They played the aria "D'Oreste, d'Ajace" from Mozart's *Idomeneo*, and a contemporary oratorio by Orazio Fiume. I had never seen an orchestra before. I couldn't believe my eyes. I learned a lot of new things about instruments, since up until then I'd only sporadically listened to the radio or heard record players. Rota played some of his own compositions for me on the piano, followed by a few passages from Alban Berg's *Wozzeck* and *Lulu*—a world that was utterly unknown to me.

Writing about my friendship with Nino Rota helps me better define his role as a composer. Indeed, many people were hostile to him because of the type of music he wrote. They didn't understand that it was simply that choosing *one* style necessarily leads to the exclusion of others, without detracting in the least from his incredibly strong qualifications (not to mention that the influences of such composers as Stravinsky, Prokofiev, and Bartók are audible in his work). What I mean to say is that, although Rota utilized one sole technique, he really did know them all. If his compositions seemed somehow less up-to-date or, to phrase it better, not exactly avant-garde, that doesn't mean he couldn't—had he so desired—have been an avant-garde composer.

CHAPTER TWO

"Have You Ever Considered Conducting?"

THE 1956–57 school year ended with a class recital in which I played Schumann's *Faschingsschwank aus Wien* (Carnival Jest from Vienna), op. 26, a rather complex piece. The performance was a success and, as it came time for me to prepare for college, it precipitated my family's decision to move to Naples. My mother, who guided us all, had been considering this for some time—my two older brothers were already there—and the whole family again turned to Rota for advice. Always an extraordinary man, he was doubly so in this case. He suggested with humble honesty that I enroll in a more important conservatory than the one in Bari—the Conservatorio San Pietro a Majella in Naples—and wrote me a letter of recommendation to its director, Jacopo Napoli. So we all moved, and I enrolled in second-year classes at the *liceo statale*[1] Vittorio Emanuele. I went back just a few months ago and the receptionist said, in dialect, "How are you, Maestro? I see you right before my eyes every day."[2] In response to my perplexed look—I hadn't set foot there since 1959—he pointed to a plaque inscribed with famous graduates' names, including Giuseppe Mercalli, inventor of the well-known seismic intensity scale; all but me were dead, and I was last on the list.

When I first arrived I met with Napoli, who handed me over to the great pianist Vincenzo Vitale for an audition. Vitale was then fifty, and incredibly cultured. I went to his house at Via Mergellina 2—with an unforgettable view of Vesuvius, boats, ships, smugglers' motorboats, and an incredible panorama outside his window—to show him how I played Schumann's op. 26. I gave it my all, and he glimpsed my performance's qualities, but he meted out harsh punishment. In terms of technique, I had to start over from scratch: I had to learn different positions and play unbelievably slowly, with the additional risk that my two brothers might well go insane after hearing me play the most basic formulas, like do-re-mi-fa, for hours on end.

Enrolling in his class was fundamental for me because, through the piano, Vitale taught not only the instrument but everything about music *tout court*. He is the one who gave me a sense of the unparalleled phrasing and agogic accent[3] perfectly outlined in the letters of the Neapolitan-influenced Austrian pianist Sigismund Thalberg and the methodologies of Beniamino Cesi and Giuseppe Martucci. For them, the phrase counted on its own; it contained its own procedural mode, and therefore precluded the fatal "Here's how I hear it" philosophy so popular among contemporary musicians who have fallen victim to the same amateurish drift that, up until then, also propelled me. For them, the phrase had its own natural, internal law; seeking to discover it and then scrupulously respect it was a sign not of frigidity but rather of objective, even scientific consideration of musical notation. For example, a musician must track down the climax, not betray it; he must clarify points of agogic accent, and reveal them. Those who, conversely, naïvely trust their own feelings often end up disrespecting the phrase and inevitably disobeying it, thereby ruining it. That's how the masters cited by Vitale saw it, and they were right.

I studied with him and made major progress. By the end of the year I was playing Liszt's *Rhapsodie espagnole* and a few of Thalberg's difficult études like a virtuoso. When the Naples conservatory organized a trip to Bari, I played one of those pieces and gained the admiration of a great organist who taught there, Armando Renzi. In Vitale's class the cult of the Neapolitan school, in the broadest sense, reigned supreme—when I walked the length of Via Caracciolo and crossed the Villa Comunale, that school was right before my eyes, so to speak; the statue of Sigismund Thalberg was the first one I met, and from there I passed an entire dynasty that ended, at the time, with Vitale.

The former Celestine convent that housed the Conservatory of San Pietro a Majella, on the other hand, was a religious place in and of itself. Its evocative, sparse classrooms emanated a feeling of *Sturm und Drang* with their feeble lightbulbs in the center of the ceiling and modest caned chairs. When I gave a concert, many years later, with the Philadelphia Orchestra at Indiana University, they showed me a piano classroom with two grand pianos, a bar, carpets, a splendid, luxurious space, and I couldn't help but marvel at how lucky the American students were— or, conversely, how lucky we had been to study in such modest rooms that had nevertheless been home to people like Giovanni Paisiello, the first illustrious director of that conservatory.

I continued going to classes at the Liceo Vittorio Emanuele, which had brilliant teachers (I remember one of the philosophy teachers in particular) but occasionally had a substitute who wasn't quite up to muster. One told us Menenius Agrippa was an "amphibious general" because he won both on land and at sea. When we raucously took issue with that, irritating him, he promised he'd have revenge: "I'll cook you all like octopus, in your own water, and slowly!" In 1959, from a class of thirty, only four or five of us earned our diploma; it was an unbelievably tough school! That year I spent less time at the conservatory in order to focus on my high school classes. I definitely missed out on a few things, but fortunately Maestro Vitale was the first to see the importance of his students' exposure to culture beyond the world of music, so he was understanding.

One day the conservatory director, Jacopo Napoli, called me in. I thought he was going to reprimand me for my absences, so I stood rigidly at attention like a toy soldier before his desk and the large portrait of Francesco Cilea hung on the wall behind him. He stared at me. "Have you ever considered conducting?" Of all the questions I might have imagined, that was the one I least expected. He added: "I heard you play at last year's recital"—I had played an expressive piece by Saint-Saëns, the *Caprice sur les airs de ballet d'Alceste de Gluck*—"and have the impression you play more like a conductor than a pianist." He meant my *forma mentis*, which, of course, I'd never thought about. "This year," he continued, "there isn't anyone in the composition class interested in conducting for the orchestral recital class. There's a monk, a priest, a woman. You have certain qualities. Why don't you give it a try?"

He had already set up an appointment with Maestro Ugo Ajello—a person I owe an enormous debt of gratitude, a fine gentleman, authentic Neapolitan, first cellist with the orchestra of the Teatro San Carlo, a great musician—who ran the orchestral recital class. They were going to play Bach's concertos for two and four harpsichords. The conservatory also had an excellent piano teacher, Tina De Maria, whose students were to play those two pieces. I met with Ajello and opened the score—fortunately it was Bach, and the only clef I found difficult was the alto, used for the viola. Ajello explained and demonstrated with his arms: "'In two' is like this, 'in four' like this; the right keeps the rhythm and the left 'the heart and soul.'" Those were his exact words. Today they might seem like a figure of speech, or a bit florid, but that's essentially right, and he taught me to demand that each hand perform a different task.

The following morning, filled with fear, I found myself standing before the students—my colleagues. I began conducting for the very first time, and I remember the spectacularly strange sensation I felt with the first beat. Later on I understood why my other great teacher, Antonino Votto, said, dropping his right arm more or less randomly, "Do this, and something will happen." For the first few minutes I was very focused on the gestures, then the movement became natural and my arms moved on their own. Maestro Ajello left the room, I found out later, to phone Maestro Napoli and inform him that a new orchestra conductor had been born. He'd glimpsed some qualities in my unfledged gestures. I conducted the final performance in Scarlatti Hall. All the students were there, it was a real celebration, and Maestro Vitale was pleased to see me, one of his pupils, in that position.

That was also when Jacopo Napoli assigned me an entire concert, a real concert, for the following year if I agreed to enroll in the composition class, which he believed was indispensable for an aspiring conductor. I put myself in the hands of the best teacher, Maestro Aladino Di Martino, who had studied with Camillo De Nardis and Gennaro Napoli. Ugo Rapalo taught me the seven different clefs and how to read the score; his system was ancient yet infallible, and to this day I can withstand even the kinds of snares set by horn players—who read in the most varied ways—when they ask what the transposed note is, just to test you.

In 1961 I earned my diploma with top scores and honors in piano. I conducted Mussorgsky's *Pictures at an Exhibition* and it seems I did it quite well. I led the student orchestra, with reinforcements brought in from the Scarlatti and San Carlo orchestras (including Giuseppe Prencipe, who went on to the Santa Cecilia Conservatory, Giacinto Caramia, and Salvatore Altobelli, all superb musicians), through a program of Beethoven's *Leonore* no. 3, Schubert's *Unfinished* Symphony, the intermezzo of Pizzetti's *Pisanella*, and Chopin's Concerto no. 1 with Laura De Fusco as the soloist. And although Schubert's symphony is a natural choice for such a concert, even if you don't have anything new to say with it, *Leonore* is another matter altogether!

I conducted it from memory: that's how I worked at the time, and I continued to do so until I met Sviatoslav Richter, who asked: "Why from memory? No eye?" (sic!). From then on I saw things differently. Those two words convinced me to always have the score on the podium: you've lived with it for months, so looking at it during the concert must mean something. Now I turn the pages even when I conduct *La forza del destino*, which I obviously know by heart; anyway, it would be absurd to change your method depending on whose work it is. The first tour stop was in Avellino, two days later. When we launched into *Leonore*, in the crescendo, at fortissimo, because the audience was basically a bunch of schoolkids, the entire hall shouted wildly; the elementary school students, taken by the explosion of music, tossed their satchels into the air.

A few months later Maestro Vitale went to teach in America for some time. There was a Roman newspaper, *Il Quotidiano*, that published a Neapolitan edition in which he reviewed the city's musical events, and upon his departure he asked me to take his place as critic for a while. I was embarrassed, because I found it difficult to go to concerts to judge rather than just to listen, and that unease had everything to do with my profession as interpreter. Nevertheless, I reviewed Massenet's *Thaïs* with Ettore Bastianini, conducted by Francesco Molinari-Pradelli, as well as many of Franco Caracciolo's concerts. Back then such a role required a tuxedo. The one I rented was too large, and it pulled me back with each step: I could barely move. Standing so still and pensive, I seemed entirely absorbed by my work as critic.

CHAPTER THREE

"Parlamme nu fesso a'a vota!"

Iɴ late 1961 Maestro Napoli accepted the directorship of the Milan Conservatory and advised me to transfer there as well. Milan, he told me, had Antonino Votto and Bruno Bettinelli, who taught orchestra conducting and composition, respectively, as well as a properly metropolitan music scene. Once again a major family meeting was convened, and my mother said yes—even if, back then, the idea of going so far away reminded everyone of famous scenes from the film *Totò, Peppino e la malafemmina.*[1] In a southern boy's imagination it could only seem a faraway, mysterious, fantastic place. I had enrolled in philosophy: I'm not a born thinker, but I thought it would help in my chosen profession by giving me a basic understanding of aesthetics. (Before that, I'd also enrolled in the musical paleography school at the musical archive of Naples, but the subject proved too difficult.)

I arrived on November 2, 1962. Had I known even a word of Milanese dialect, I'd have said, "L'è el dì di mort, alegher!" (It's the Day of the Dead, rejoice!).[2] Mom and Dad had prepared me for the trip with a litany of abominable remarks, exactly like Totò in Mastrocinque's film: "Listen, it's cold up there, Milan is foggy, you'll catch pneumonia." They even bought me a Borsalino hat—I'd never worn one in my life, and it made me think of

Vittorio Gassman's famous line in *Il Sorpasso* (*The Easy Life*), a film that had come out that year: "Look out, gramps, or you'll lose your Borsalino!"[3] as well as a little poem by Ettore Petrolini: "È importante ricordarsi / che si parte domattin: / sarìa triste allontanarsi / senza avere il Borsalin")[4]—plus a wool scarf. I arrived alone, got off the train, and immediately thought of Totò and De Filippo's huge fur hats; I'd just gotten used to Naples, and this new city was so different that the only thing missing was polar bears! I went to the Verdi Conservatory and it made an odd impression on me. Its facade was small and low, giving no hint of the vast cloister just inside, and it was utterly unlike San Pietro a Majella. I enrolled and soon met Bettinelli, and I took classes in organ accompaniment with Achille Schinelli and in score reading with Riccardo Castagnone, with whom I played countless duets.

And then there was Votto, whom I recall so vividly. He was solemn and incredibly strict, and had worked with Toscanini during his years at La Scala. The homey southern world—in the best sense of those terms: the southern muse—nurtured by my dear maestro Ajello, was gone; my new maestro, Votto, instead flaunted a Toscaninian detachment and coolness that contrasted, if you'll pardon a cliché, with the "hot" environment I'd experienced at the foot of Vesuvius. When I met him he said: "You're Muti? Take *Don Giovanni*, study the overture, then come back and show me what you've got." Those were his first words, and I had no choice but to obey. A week later in Puccini Hall, with the students before me, I began.

With Mozart's grand overture, it takes real skill to "separate" the andante of the slow introduction from the molto allegro that follows. There were some difficulties: I can't recall whether the uncertainties were my own or those of the orchestra kids, but after three tries my annoyance was beginning to show and, as I was about to convey that to them by behaving like a career conductor rather than the student I was, I raised my left hand and felt someone behind me grab it. It was Votto; he'd climbed a few stairs and was at my back. I tried to say something, but he interrupted me. "Parlamme nu fesso a'a vota!" he said in Neapolitan dialect: "Let's talk one dolt at a time!" I saw a look of Schadenfreude cross the orchestra musicians' faces as I, the conductor, was held up to public scorn. "It's your fault. Look." He brushed me aside and calmly led the passage. The reasons it went smoothly were basic: On the one hand, he was Antonino Votto; on the other, the kids gave it their all just to show me who the "dolt" was. I was completely disheartened. In Naples I'd conducted a triumphant concert, and here in Milan it was hard to sufficiently separate an allegro. I was afraid this would be just like my work with Vitale and the piano, that I'd have to start all over again from scratch.

Within a few days, however, I realized that Votto had taken a liking to me, to the point of giving me—as if to prefer me over less talented students, or ones he didn't like as much—some pieces to conduct for the performances the following year. Not only did I take a class with him, but I also attended some of his rehearsals at La Scala. In order to avoid running into people, he steered clear of Via Filodrammatici and entered from Via Verdi, in his trademark gray overcoat; once in the hall, he'd hand it to the orchestra inspector and climb to the podium to rehearse. I was particularly struck when he did *Falstaff*: he didn't have the score! Now, it's one thing to conduct from memory, but to try

that with *Falstaff* is one of those things that just leaves you flab-
bergasted and makes you think that maybe, with such experts
around, you'd best find another job. I asked him something along
those lines, and he replied: "If you had worked with Him, you
would do the same." "Him," of course, meant Toscanini, with
whom such work was an intense, special, months-long undertaking; after that, going on memory became spontaneous, the
natural result of having complete mastery of the score.

I also have fond memories of Bettinelli's composition
and counterpoint classes. My class included outstanding students like Armando Gentilucci, Azio Corghi, and Francesco
Degrada. Francesco was also taking the orchestral recital class
with me, but he was a better historian than conductor. In one
of Cimarosa's symphonies, where the meter was marked 2/4, he
insisted on conducting 4/4. Votto impatiently yelled out: "Two-
four, two-four!"

Francesco coolly replied, "I hear it this way."

Votto, keeping his anger in check: "Do as you wish,
hardhead!"

I had a great friendship with Corghi, and we had endless
counterpoint competitions. I still have notebooks filled with
exercises on the canon, *rectus, inversus*, through increase (*aggra-
vamento*), through decrease (*diminuzione*), as if we were two
young Flemings.[5] Classmates told me Corghi sometimes said,
"Riccardo was better than I was!" I think he said that out of
friendship or pity, because I was good, but he was really first-
rate, so my supposed primacy was entirely unfounded.

In 1963 I conducted a concert in Verdi Hall with the conservatory orchestra and chorus; it was the same concert we

performed later as an homage to Pope Paul VI, who had just previously been archbishop of Milan. We played Vivaldi's *Magnificat* and Scarlatti's *Stabat Mater*.

*

One day, during a rehearsal with the instumental group in Puccini Hall, the doors opened with an unbelievably loud noise and a girl burst in skipping, as she expected to find the chorus rehearsal there. I was a student, true, but up on the podium I wore the garb of an "authority"—that is, let's just say, I exhibited the author-ity of a maestro. And so, with an imperious gesture, I signaled to her that she should leave. The young lady I was sending away was Cristina Mazzavillani, who would become my wife on June 1, 1969, and who at the time was in Maria Carbone's singing class. When she asked around to see who I was, people replied, "Il Moro," the Moor. Because of my thick black hair, and maybe a vein of racism since I came from the South, that's how I was known at the conservatory. We met soon thereafter. They'd told her who "the Moor" was, assured her I was no Othello, and added that I was always rather sullen and wore a hat.

That had been true since I'd moved north—remember Petrolini's line "it would be sad to go . . . "—but I stopped wear-ing it one day after I ran into an old friend, Domenico D'Aquino. Domenico was working for a telephone company to make ends meet while he studied classical guitar at the conservatory. We knew each other from Naples, and that morning when our paths crossed in the lobby, he remarked in his heavy accent, "Hey, Rick, whadja do to yourself? You look like Barièllo."[6] I couldn't help but ask who this Barièllo was, and he smugly replied, "That guy who's always wearing a hat."[7] I took it off that instant and never put it back on, not even when it was forty below outside. That was the inglorious end of all my mom's comments about the Borsalino, the cold, pneumonia, and polar bears at the train station!

D'Aquino was an incredible guy. One time he even managed to make Votto smile. We were at the front desk of the conservatory, and Votto walked up and in his typically austere voice asked the receptionist: "A taxi"—long pause—"please."

"Maestro, my car's right outside," said D'Aquino in dialect. "I'll give you a ride home."

Votto replied: "I only take"—slightly shorter pause—"cars"—another pause—"for hire."

D'Aquino promptly replied: "What, you thought I was gonna give you a ride for nothin'?"

And Votto laughed—for once!

After that, I realized he was a little slice of Naples transplanted into the strict *lumbard* conservatory. This was an entirely different world, but having Votto there was good for me—despite our differences—because it continued my exposure to a strictness that was in many ways similar to the one I'd known in the South. The only thing missing was the sense of humor I'd experienced throughout my teen years. For me, being Apulian—or rather an Apulo-Campanian—living in Milan and studying at the conservatory meant living in an almost Austro-Hungarian environment of silent discipline.

I went ahead with the class performances and concerts for the San Fedele Cultural Center, where Lorenzo Arruga was artistic director. I remember that on one occasion I conducted Chopin's Concerto no. 2 in F minor with Maria Luisa Caprara on piano. We also played some contemporary pieces, including compositions by students like Umberto Rotondi. Meanwhile I followed rehearsals at La Scala and RAI.[8] I particularly remember Lovro von Matačić, who conducted Beethoven's symphonies, and Sergiu Celibidache's rehearsals. For one class performance I composed a piano piece and played it in Puccini Hall. Its style was incredibly difficult, modern, and complicated, and was modeled on the style we had studied in Bettinelli's class. I looked at my score again a few days ago and it showed how time flies. Nowadays I wouldn't be able to play even three beats of a piece like that!

During my last year at the conservatory we prepared an opera that we then performed at the Teatro dell'Arte. A few faculty musicians, including Paolo Borciani, first violin of the Quartetto Italiano, and Luigi Ferro, performed with the student orchestra. We played Paisiello's *L'osteria di Marechiaro* in an arrangement by Jacopo Napoli, and the singers were chosen from Maria Carbone's students (Cristina sang the part of Lesbina). That was the first opera I ever conducted. We even took it briefly on tour. The following year we did two more operas: Donizetti's *Rita* and Jacopo Napoli's *Il rosario*, which starred Cristina and which was a major success in Lugano, where the radio was headquartered.

In 1966 I graduated with top grades, and to earn a living I accepted a post as accompanying pianist for Maria Carbone's class.

*

It hadn't been easy to find housing in Milan. Early on I stayed at a humble hotel on the Piazza Cinque Giornate, and then I heard about a priest who knew someone who had an apartment

for rent. I walked to the castle, then out toward the neighborhood near the trade fair center, and with large suitcase in hand
I knocked on the door. They'd rented it out the day before. I
retraced my steps all the way to that humble little hotel on foot,
and they took me back in. After Christmas vacation the conservatory receptionist, a disabled man from Calabria who was quite
fond of me, sent me to a little old lady from Vicenza who lived at
Via Tadino 2. She smoked a carton of cigarettes a day and gave
me a room with two twin beds. "A tenor, Mr. Mamprin, sleeps in
the other one," she said. "He's out singing tonight." For the first
time in my life, I went to bed without knowing who would show
up later that night. The next morning I awoke to find a huge guy
just a few feet from me; we introduced ourselves and became
friends. But he spent his days doing vocal exercises, so in order
not to get too confused, I had to stick to writing out counterpoint
notations, bundled up just like Totò,[9] on a bench in the park near
Porta Venezia. I stayed there a year, and the tenor took the oil
my dad sent up from Apulia like a miracle cure.

Later on I found a room of my own on Via Pindemonte
in a building where two old ladies lived, one a singer, the other
a harpist. When they were younger, their company had toured
South America; the world they inhabited seemed straight out
of Verdi, it was so old-fashioned. I stayed there until I finished
my diploma, and regularly ate out with Cristina and a few of
her girlfriends at a restaurant on Viale Premuda, a small tavern
where lunch cost 400 lire; today it's a bit more up-to-date. When
I began working as a piano accompanist with Carbone—who
was already a famous singer, especially known for "realist"
opera,[10] and an excellent teacher as well, from whom I learned

a lot about both singers' voices and their techniques—I found a room (with a shower, a relative luxury) just across from the conservatory. I furnished it with my winnings from the 1967 Cantelli Competition and suddenly found myself in a nice living room with a piano; I felt my dreams had come true. The following year I won a tenured position as pianist and felt my life had hit its high point now that I'd settled both my workspace and living arrangements.

*

In order to participate in the Cantelli Competition, an important contest open to emerging young conductors, you had to practice. The proposed works included Beethoven, Brahms, and Stravinsky, a repertoire with which I'd had almost no experience, and opportunities of the sort were unheard of in Italy. Luckily an old baroness who lived in a splendid palazzo on Via del Gesù, Dorothy Lanni della Quara, president of the Gioventù Musicale d'Italia (Young Italian Musicians organization), had taken an interest in me. She came to hear performances at the conservatory and I caught her eye. To help me find a way to get the necessary practice, in September 1966 she sent me to Prague to conduct a chamber symphony orchestra in a barracks. (In such barracks in Italy you'd find a small brass band at best, but there they had a complete orchestra.) All alone and far from home, "behind the Iron Curtain" as we said back then, I stayed at a tiny hotel, and to keep my morale up and homesickness at bay I took nightly walks past the Italian Embassy just around the corner.

I worked with the military musicians on a series of concerts in northern Italy for the Gioventù Musicale events we played in such towns as Thiene and Carpi. The program included Dvořák's

New World Symphony, Tchaikovsky's Fifth, Beethoven's *Leonore* no. 3 and the prisoners' chorus from *Fidelio*, and a Brahms rhapsody. It took great effort, as it was my first time, but it gave me the chance to resolve a whole host of problems, even ones related to the basic aspects of arm "gestures," in an environment and with a repertoire that, for historical and geographic reasons, the musicians before me were completely familiar with. Their presence felt invaluable, as I kept Antonino Votto's absolute rule in mind: abstract gestures and practice in front of a mirror are useless; the arms are an extension of the mind and, once you master the basic movements, their motion must be entirely spontaneous, as if they were purely an extension of your thoughts. That's how I've always conducted, in an entirely natural way, and I've never had to stop and think, what do I do now?—not even when I conducted *The Rite of Spring* with the Philadelphia Orchestra. Sure, the technique is based on scientific rules all conductors know, and some may have read about them in Hermann Scherchen's manual, but, speaking for myself, I've never done any scientific study of it.

The most important stop was Bergamo, at the Teatro Donizetti. I wasn't even thirty yet, and it was like playing Carnegie Hall or Berlin's Philharmonie! And all of it helped me get my conducting arm in shape for the upcoming competition. The jury included Votto, Ferrara, Efrem Kurtz, Segnini, Napoli, and a few others. I won, and two days later, on October 1, 1967, I conducted Beethoven's Seventh and Verdi's *Vespers* at the Teatro Coccia in Novara. All my relatives came, but before I began, my mother gave them all strict orders not to applaud. She was from an unbelievably rigid family, and viewed clapping for a relative an inconsiderate weakness. My father, on the other hand, had the same open, warm, and cordial temperament as my roommate the tenor, and visibly wanted to clap.

That competition led to two invitations, one from Catania, one from Genoa. Back then the media weren't nearly what they are today, so it was more difficult to make a living with music, and more difficult to become known. The plans for Genoa fell through because the director wanted complete control over the program and I wanted some say. I didn't balk out of impertinence, but rather out of rigor: I was very young and, because I didn't yet have my own repertoire, I preferred to establish myself with works I had a firm handle on.

But the Catania concert did take place. I conducted the *New World Symphony* and one of Bellini's two symphonies in E-flat, plus a piece by Renato Parodi, an elegant Neapolitan conductor and excellent scorer and music arranger. My flight from Milan arrived in the evening, and I went straight to the theater, where the intense scent of orange blossoms from the surrounding countryside overtook me. This was the town of Mignon, the "land where lemon trees blossom" evoked by Goethe: it was like a drug, its effect was so strong. As I walked past the musicians' entrance, the receptionist welcomed me and handed me one of the beers he'd just ordered. I've often reflected, since then, on how different the world I'm from can be—it's deeply Italian, Mediterranean, "southern"—how it can still be, despite its well-known defects, quite marvelous. Traveling the globe, I've never found receptionists of this sort. They usually embody their role in the worst ways, and some have been even more severe than their institutions' director.

Our rehearsal days were marvelous. The orchestra was warm and passionate, even though it was no Chicago Symphony. I still remember how, at the end of Dvořák's *New World*, when the music culminates with an E-sharp and the strings' tremolo,[11] I felt something move to my right. I looked over and saw the first cello, Mr. Paladino, standing and signaling for even more enthusiasm and participation from the orchestra; it was as if we were conducting together! Such individual character used to be common, and might not be so prevalent today—we've all become more "the same," more composed. At the end of the overall rehearsal I still had a few doubts about certain passages and wasn't entirely satisfied, but he came up to reassure me: "Maestro, you needn't worry, the evening of the concert we'll be the Berliner Philharmoniker."

In the final months of 1967 I also went to Montreux, Switzerland, and to the Pomeriggi Musicali (Musical Afternoons) in Milan, led at the time by Remigio Paone, whom I would soon know well as a theater manager in Florence.

CHAPTER FOUR

The Performer?

I N March 1968, Remigio Paone invited me to Florence to conduct a concert where the soloist was none other than Sviatoslav
Richter, a veritable giant compared to me. Since I was entirely
unknown at the time, they requested his approval, and he in turn
requested that I meet him in Siena, where he was preparing a
recital for the Accademia Chigiana. I understood he wanted to
test me, to find out what kind of musician I was. He'd ask me
to play, and so I intensively studied the piano reduction of each
orchestral score with which I was to accompany him. The works
were Mozart's Piano Concerto in B-flat, K. 450, and Britten's
Piano Concerto in D Major, a powerful piece in five movements.
I went to Siena and met him at the academy. In a large music
hall I saw the towering Richter waiting for me in front of two
pianos. He had me play the Mozart along with him, taking the
part of the orchestra. We went on to play the Britten, with the
same division of labor. At the end he stood up and said, through
his interpreter: "If you conduct the same way you play, you are a
good musician. I agree to perform the concert with you."

I arrived in Florence and found myself standing before the
Orchestra del Maggio,[1] an ensemble with a great reputation. But
an impending strike brought chaos and a certain revelry with it,

and all the misbehavior that entails; they were slow to notice I was on the podium, as if I were just there to witness their chatter rather than to conduct.

We began with the *Sea Interludes* from Britten's *Peter Grimes*, followed by Mozart's Symphony in C Major, K. 338, and the two concertos by Mozart and Britten. At each pause between works, debate arose among the musicians, and at a certain point I began to show my impatience with such disorder. The orchestra quieted and—since they also happened to be looking for a principal conductor—some of them began to consider me. Their interest in me grew during the second rehearsal. On the third day the concert was canceled because of the strike. Yet Paone, who was a sharp impresario, decided to reschedule the concert for the following May.

The strike ended up working in my favor. The orchestra had already taken an interest in me, and come May, I figured, they'd be looking to see whether their positive first impressions were justified. And that's precisely what happened: the atmosphere was completely different—calm and collaborative during the rehearsals, enthusiastic during the concert. In his review, Florentine critic Leonardo Pinzauti wrote: "A very young, surprising orchestra conductor has brought a glimmer of hope to our hearts."[2]

Paone then booked me again for the following October. After beginning with Ghedini's *Appunti per un Credo*, I did Mozart's Concerto for Clarinet K. 622, (with Detalmo Corneti, the local first clarinet, as soloist), and in the second half Richard Strauss's *Aus Italien*. As I mentioned, the orchestra's enthusiasm was at fever pitch, to the point where Piero Farulli, a member

of the board, unexpectedly showed up to see if all the talk he'd
heard about me was well founded.

After that concert in Florence, Pinzauti wrote that "the
enthusiasm . . . appeared more than justified, such that it also
left some good hope regarding the age-old question of finding a 'principal conductor.'"[3] The theater managers offered me
the position, and I began in early 1969. The orchestra actually
pushed in favor of my being hired, and the extraordinary offer
put me in a state of distress. Indeed, that institution was pres-
tigious enough to make any conductor as young as I was feel
a bit apprehensive. Its collaborators included Paone, Luciano
Alberti, and the marvelous Renato Mariani, who was the theater's secretary general. Roman Vlad was also there, as he'd
been brought in to organize the Maggio Musicale festival with
an "expressionist" theme, which was a success. That was the
same period when Zubin Mehta had begun performing as vis-
iting conductor in Florence (he did an intriguing *Aida* with
Shirley Verrett). The fact that many different people took part
in the festival although their roles weren't yet well defined is
indicative of the extraordinary innovative transition the theater
was going through.

And so I became "principal conductor," the conductor who
"stayed put" at the theater and managed its seasons without traveling abroad much. That was the task and the label, since the title
"music director" didn't exist yet. (That role comes from Anglo-
Saxon culture, but in Italy bestows less authority. Especially in
America, the music director is at the top of the power pyramid
in organizations without a bureaucratic system parallel to the
Italian one.)

As soon as I was nominated, I went to the Ceccherini music store, which was still in its old location on Via Tornabuoni, and bought *my own* piano, a Schimmel baby grand that has been with me my entire career since 1969, and on which I still prepare my performances to this day. I'd never have the courage to cheat on it with a Steinway grand piano, say, or any other for that matter, because I literally consider it a "person" with whom I carry out for hours on end the marvelous dialogue Schubert so perfectly captured in his modest and sublime "An mein Klavier." I had them send it to the house Cristina and I lived in at number 8 Via Rucellai, next to the American Episcopal church of Saint James.

We had married in Ravenna on June 1 that year, in the ancient Chiesa di Sant'Agata. My best man was Maestro Votto, while Sviatoslav Richter became our ad hoc photographer and took some of the best photos. Nino Rota showed up at the cere-mony in a taxi, carrying an empty leather trunk he'd had branded with my initials. It was empty, he said, because I was to fill it up with my life experiences. We spent the evening at the Circolo degli amici (the Circle of Friends, a group of buddies who adored operatic melodrama and good cooking) with Dino Ciani, Maria Carbone, and Jacopo Napoli, among others. After din-ner an almost spontaneous musical duel arose between Rota and Richter, who took turns at the piano to play increasingly shorter bits of the repertoire while the other had to guess what piece it was. As the competition ended up with the two playing ever "rarer" titles, Richter displayed an ability and breadth of knowl-edge that amazed many of us; the capabilities of the super-Italian Rota were beyond question, but that night we learned that, in his youth, Richter had been a piano accompanist at an opera house.

*

The Maggio Musicale Fiorentino festival was founded by Vittorio Gui, who launched it with a symphonic concert on the afternoon of April 30, 1933. He was an extraordinary figure and deserves greater consideration, given everything he did for music (for example, his major dedication to bringing some of Rossini's operas back to the stage, or his great symphonic repertoire, from Brahms on). The ideas that led to the birth of that festival were incredibly advanced, and not just for the thirties. It was ushered in by an international congress that began April 30 of that year and included, in addition to all the Italians, such high-caliber historians as Paul Bekker and Edward Dent—already evidence enough that the initiative was anything but provincial.[4] They staged Bellini's *I puritani* with sets by De Chirico, Spontini's *La vestale* with sketches by Felice Casorati, and Donizetti's *Lucrezia Borgia* with sketches by Mario Sironi, putting on programs that were futuristic compared to the way melodrama was usually done in Italy back then, often shaped strictly by the theaters' need for survival.

Forty years later, Gui's enduring presence in the city was quite important for me as well. Today no one remembers him, with the exception of a few vinyl fanatics, so no one knows about his many performances at the Glyndebourne Festival, to name just one example. There he showed Rossini in a witty, classy way that was radically different from the overwrought comedy of those who used the *opera buffa* repertoire only to turn it into a string of vulgarities and crass gags—a trend quickly and most unfortunately taken up in Germany as well. Just think of what they manage to do with the refined *Don Pasquale*, transforming it into a bungled joke of an opera; the audience doesn't laugh at the light, cultured comedy of the libretto and music, but instead falls prey to the low tricks played by the singers and director in their complete distortion of the work. Gui had immense cultural depth. When I met him in Fiesole, in a house brimming with musical artifacts (he knew Richard Strauss, among others), he conjured up the major figures of recent musical history with such immediacy and vivacity that I felt as if I'd known them myself. Even in his personal life he had an acute critical sense of the people and circumstances of the Italian music world, so his opinions and personality sometimes differed from the official opinions now published in books.

Through Gui I met the composer Luigi Dallapiccola. We were having lunch with Vlad, and a lively debate—an argument, really—sprang up between Vlad and Dallapiccola. The latter was leveling severe judgment against some important twentieth-century artists, tossing Brahms, Shostakovich, and Tchaikovsky together, and treating them like dirt, of course. When it came to Brahms, Gui, who'd clearly run out of patience, signaled to me. I leaned over and he began to whisper; he was utterly entitled to, because he unabashedly referred to himself—with a heightened, yet endearing, not at all arrogant sense of self-worth—as "the apostle of Brahms." For ages already, ever since 1922, when he published an article titled "Brahms primo dei moderni" (Brahms, First among the Moderns), he'd railed against those who believed they "could do just fine without realizing the great importance of his music."[5]

His closeness was also important for me because he led me toward a musical world that was the exact opposite of

Votto's, the sole source from which I'd drawn until then. Votto's approach was based on conductorial efficiency, music for music's sake, no frills, no bells and whistles, going straight to the heart of opera, only essential gestures, nothing more than was absolutely necessary. In his classes he'd often repeat, "Don't annoy the orchestra." To the uninitiated that phrase might seem absurd or misleading, calling into question the orchestra conductor's usefulness. In reality he just wanted to advise us that, once the orchestra was on an orderly, rhythmic path (the obvious outcome of long rehearsing), the maestro mustn't disturb that natural gait, and must therefore avoid rash gestures while on the podium, steering clear of any temptation to become a court jester; basically, he mustn't alter what the nature of the piece itself had established. And such a position was a clear, complete reflection of Arturo Toscanini's.

Well, in Gui this efficiency was transformed into images wherein *culture* was predominant; he called them "stages along a line of thought that always closely supports the work of the interpreter" (and performer), and posed us an evidently rhetorical question: "What is the interpreter if not a critic knocking on the doors of all creation?"[6] In his dealings with the orchestra he was a highly cultured person, and for him the importance of the gesture was secondary. Indeed, nobody remembers him being a technical virtuoso. But in the field of symphonic music he had an irreplaceable role. We mustn't forget that at the time Italy still had to (and perhaps still *has* to) make a remarkable effort to regain the symphonic, chamber-orchestral sensibility that the vogue for melodrama had swept aside in the public consciousness. The phenomenon goes way back: Musicians like Giuseppe

Martucci and Giovanni Sgambati, even Ottorino Respighi, eked out a meager living and remained in the shadows because they nobly insisted on trying to steer Italy back to the European tradition it had clearly lost sight of by identifying solely with opera, which is both the blessing and the curse of our musical culture. Gui, on the other hand, regularly did Brahms, Beethoven, and even Bach, Handel, Cherubini, and Spontini. Sure, he did so with the attitude of the time, free of any modern, formal scrupulousness—for example, he didn't hesitate to cut the *Vestale*—but he nevertheless did so with extraordinarily close examination. Even with Spontini's *Agnes von Hohenstaufen*: When I took it up in 1974, I was convinced it was a miraculous rediscovery, only to find that it had already been done, right there in Florence, by Gui in 1954. Needless to say, his was an extremely reduced version compared to the original. We spoke about it, and he told me that the second act should be considered a masterpiece from the first to the very last note, as those were some of the nineteenth century's most beautiful pages of musical score.

It was thus at Gui's house that I began to reflect on conducting as a question not only of accuracy and precision but of great culture as well. I had intuited this when I matriculated in philosophy, but only Gui helped me become fully aware of its implications.

*

Of course, in Florence I conducted both concerts and operas. Before the Maggio Musicale festival season began, I had already done *I puritani* at the RAI auditorium in Rome. I'd been invited there by Francesco Siciliani, a key figure in my artistic growth (he'd spotted me in Milan when I was at the conservatory, as he was creative director at La Scala). The first opera I did in Florence was *I masnadieri* (The Bandits) in the winter of 1969, with a preset cast in an interesting directorial revival by Erwin Piscator, which was very modern for the time. It was also my first Verdi done "on stage." I didn't have any trouble controlling the large stage and the hall's imperfect acoustics. I immediately got the feeling the audience was fantastic. To this day, that particular audience remains one of the most extraordinary of all the ones I've met over the span of my entire life in music, in the most varied places in the world. That audience followed me for twelve years, standing by me and believing in me. I'll especially never forget its warm reception of *I Puritani,* beginning with the performance given on December 1, 1970.[7]

That audience understood everything I brought to the stage, such as Rossini's *Guillaume Tell* (William Tell) in the original, full-length version, directed by Mario Sequi with sets by Pier Luigi Pizzi. It was a demanding piece, especially when it came to finding the right person to play the role of Arnold Melchtal. I called Nicolai Gedda, and although he was no longer so young, he nevertheless undertook the enormous task. It would only be for two performances. The piece ran from eight in the evening to two in the morning, and the audience didn't hide its astonishment when he attacked the final climax and theme (which RAI used at the end of its television programming), becoming the embodiment of an authentic resurrection. At the dress rehearsal, indeed, when the marvelous C major sounded at the end and the whole theater lit up in white, at the first stand a cellist named Balducci held his instrument up and shouted, "Viva Rossini, viva l'Italia!" in an outpouring of the joy he felt at belonging, as a musician, to such a superb world. I'll never forget that. The following performances brought out people's enthusiasm, and that Florentine audience, intelligent as it was, never worried too much about analyzing whether or not the performer's voice (as of the third performance Arnold was sung by Bruno Sebastian) was exactly suited to the role. When we did it again in 1976, I chose Franco Bonisolli, and a few vocal experts objected, but at the time I wanted to expose that masterpiece of an opera to broader public attention. I too knew how to decide how "Rossinian" any given voice was (or not). Maybe Bonisolli's execution carried a vocal weight that wasn't necessarily what Rossini had in mind, but even that's hard to say—who knows? maybe if he'd heard it he'd have liked it. The same complex problem arises when I sit down at the piano to play Bach, or when I have to decide the "correct" number of musicians to use. Mozart once wrote to his father that he was happy to have found an ensemble with twelve double basses and eight bassoons, and in the months following the debut of Haydn's *Creation* in Vienna the work was performed with a thousand musicians. Today we go overboard about just counting the numbers, associating classical style with a drastic reduction of the ensemble's size, often naïvely giving up more than is called for.[8] Back then it was important to me that the singers had their notes and that I wouldn't be forced to lower the tonality or cut anything. My perspective matched Fedele D'Amico's: with the cuts restored, *Guillaume Tell* ends up "creating the impression that the opera is shorter than usual."[9]

The first year, we also played outside Florence, traveling to Volterra, Fucecchio, and other towns throughout the region to perform Beethoven's Seventh and Verdi's *Quattro pezzi sacri* (Four Sacred Pieces). In Volterra we played the Verdi, with almost 200 performers onstage and just 37 people in the audience! Elsewhere, in the ticket booth of an old cinema the poster for *Ursus nella valle dei leoni* kept us company.[10] We weren't just paying our dues—rather, we were bringing music to the people, with the utmost dedication, even with an audience of five. I strode to the podium with the same enthusiasm as when I joined the orchestra at the Villa Comunale: *Tolle siparium*, I said to myself, repeating a useful sentence I'd read in Gluck's famous preface, *sufficit mihi unus Plato pro cuncto populo*.[11] I have the impression that, back then, people felt inspired by the possibility of creating what's often simplistically referred to as "a better world." We were at a crossroads, and as soon as we moved on, some of those roads were closed to us. Italy was trying to conquer its own remote areas by bringing them culture. The orchestra's spirit was happy—if I may use that word—as if a new paradise were opening up before it.

Siciliani had some recommendations regarding what we played at the Sagra Musicale Umbra festival (Handel's *Deborah*, Bach's *Magnificat*, Vivaldi's *Gloria*, Cherubini's Requiem in D Minor, and Mendelssohn's *Paulus*), which we also played in Florence. Meanwhile my repertoire was growing by leaps and bounds. I did *Das Lied von der Erde*, the second work by Mahler I'd done, following *Lieder eines fahrenden Gesellen*, which I'd done in Bologna with Maureen Forrester, a singer who had worked with Bruno Walter and brought to her collaboration with me—still a relatively young conductor—her extraordinary historic experiences and memories.

I did Prokofiev's *Ivan the Terrible* and *Alexander Nevsky*, as well as Meyerbeer's *L'Africaine*. All had been suggestions of the creative director, Roman Vlad, who had a fundamental influence on me because I felt his personality was the ideal combination of the cultured intellectual, the great musician, and the thoroughly prepared musicologist. I had already read his book on Stravinsky,[12] and his characteristic intellectual curiosity was truly exemplary. When Vlad spoke about Meyerbeer, he was just a name to me, despite his fame (in late nineteenth-century France his popularity was often compared to that of the cinema), and Vlad did everything he could to convince me of his significance. One rainy, windy night when I was holed up in my little pink house on Via Rucellai studying, the doorbell rang: it was Vlad. He ran up the stairs in his camel-colored Montgomery duffle coat, went to the piano room, opened the score to the page he'd chosen, and began playing his favorite passages of *L'Africaine*, including the marvelous opening of the third act, the one representing daybreak over the calm sea. I was virtually speechless, but when he left after that half-hour spent conjuring a musical tempest at the piano, he'd convinced me that it was enough of a masterpiece that we couldn't *not* do it. I set myself to studying it, and we performed it in April 1971, directed by Franco Enriquez (with whom I wanted to work again after the months we'd spent together on Scarlatti's *Dirindina*).

The piece debuted with Veriano Luchetti and Jessye Norman. Ms. Norman was larger than life, and when she stepped onstage the audience seemed surprised—but as soon as she opened her mouth to sing the aria "Figlio del sol, mio dolce amor," the audience's reaction shifted to a unanimous, amazed admiration. She had, if I may, a voice of pure chocolate, of such intense, warm, mellow beauty that it's unlike any I've heard since. Unfortunately the horrendous old Italian translation didn't do the beautiful finale justice: "su bianca nuvoletta / un cigno là mi aspetta / sul carro di cristal" (o'er yon white cloud / a swan awaits me / on a crystal chariot); you can still find recordings of that version today.

The audience's refined, cultured silence that evening (that audience loved its theater, and expressed its pride without indulging in any capriciousness) gave way to the sheer pleasure of due recognition when Veriano Luchetti launched into the famous "O paradiso dall'onde uscito," the only aria that's still performed frequently, as every tenor in the world awards it a special place in the repertoire. Indeed, it's probably responsible for a good portion of the kids named Vasco; when I lived in Tuscany I read more than one obituary of an eighty-something named Nelusko, a sure sign of the opera's success.

*

After the general unrest of 1968–69 things remained at flash point, and there was even a bit of obscurantist cultural closed-mindedness. For example, when Vlad and I chose Mascagni's *Cavalleria rusticana* and Leoncavallo's *Pagliacci* for the winter 1970–71 season, the town council held a special meeting and threatened to raise a fuss because we'd included operas that, according to them, were so negative and of such scant artistic merit. Those were tough times: there were controversies and articles in the press, and these important works of operatic realism, performed worldwide because they're deep in the public's heart, were tripped up by obstructionists interested solely in toeing the party line.

We brought them to the stage, under the direction of Mauro Bolognini. In the Leoncavallo the great (albeit slightly older) Richard Tucker played Canio, and it felt like he'd brought all the discipline of the late Toscanini with him from New York. He showed up at every rehearsal in a tie, a double-breasted black jacket, and a dark hat that he took off as soon as he set foot in the theater. A few years later, when we did Verdi's *Un ballo in maschera* together and I let him prolong one of his notes, he got up from his seat to thank me for granting him permission.

At the very beginning Tucker asked me: "Maestro, am I the one who says 'La commedia è finita'?" I told him yes, even though he'd never let me hear it during our rehearsals at the piano. It's only natural, I thought—when they get to those words, tenors always aim for utter cataclysm, they grab onto the curtain and tear it down, shouting "La commedia ... è finiiiitaaaa!" Bolognini had agreed with me in advance that we'd let Tucker dive into a few of the historically prized features of an approach to "theater" that was long gone even then— every once in a while it's nice to enjoy them as the relics of a lost tradition. At the time I didn't know that, in Leoncavallo's original, that phrase is written for baritone, which makes a lot more sense. Indeed, the Prelude is an entirely metaphysical character who appears *before* the opera, before the line "Incominciate ..."; therefore, as with the beginning, when it's all over this "non-character" character has to make his come-back and coolly recite the line "La commedia ..." without any expression whatsoever. Evidently there must have been some-one—Caruso or someone else, who knows?—who protested: "What? I sang the whole opera but I don't get to finish it? What kind of tenor do you take me for?" Hence the tradition of the tenor singing the end was born.

That's a grave mistake, like putting an acute on "Incominciate." It's the same kind of error, because there's nothing linking the metaphysical role of the character to the vocal showiness of the comeback, when the singer is stuck between curtain and audience. He has to pronounce it—and that's the right word—in an unspectacular way. Of course, it's a known fact that corrections of this sort irritate a certain kind of audience and take it out of its comfort zone. I'm of the opinion that it's fine if, in homage to certain vocal traditions, one wants to satisfy their expectations, but it's absurd to punish those who honor the author's intentions. Over time such effect-driven choices would end up becoming more important than the opera as it's written. Again, the baritone at the end of the opera has to say his line cynically, *pianissimo* and—it's written in the score—*senza rigore*, "without severity," thereby reconnecting it to the prelude, where "incominciate" isn't a G-natural but a D, just as Leoncavallo, a refined, cultured, highly educated composer, conceived of it.

Gianfranco Cecchele and Elena Souliotis sang in *Cavalleria rusticana*. The performance was greatly anticipated, and the theater was full of people who'd come up from Livorno to celebrate the work of Mascagni, their "hometown boy." The prelude that evening was just marvelous, and the set gave the piece a uniquely Mediterranean melancholy, with people surrendering to their fatigue, hard labor, and poverty, yet still enveloped in warmth. Then, all of a sudden, the performance was interrupted by a man in a trench coat whose heavy steps led straight up to the prompter, where he shouted out: "People of Florence, while you're here having fun, out in Careggi[13] people are dying of euthanasia!" An avalanche of sound arose from the crowd as people yelled, "Go away!"; it must've sounded just like what happened when ancient Roman emperors gave the thumbs-down sign during games at the Circus Maximus. I had left the podium, and because all this unfolded as Cecchele was concluding the "Siciliana," the unlucky tenor thought those shouts were aimed at him and asked the understudies at his side in the wings if he'd really sung that badly! I wanted to "delete" the whole episode and start the opera over from the very beginning. Cecchele initially disagreed, but then decided in favor of that, so we did it all over again, from the very first note.

My father was in the audience, too. He'd come up from Molfetta just to hear me conduct music he adored. But as he sat beside Cristina, he relentlessly repeated a distressed soliloquy of sorts: "That's not how it goes, my boy, that's not how it goes!" I mention this because it reflects what I was trying to do with scores of that sort. Since they'd often been massacred over the years with truly awful "effects" and usually useless overdoses of realism, I was trying to bring them back to the nobility they still have hidden inside. (Yes, the nobility they *have*. Whoever wrote that Karajan had "nobilized" Mascagni during his time at La Scala was way off, because that stylistic modesty is a natural, integral part of the *Cavalleria*, as a quick read of Bastianelli's *Mascagni* would convince anyone.)[14] Afterward he only said, with a typically kind, affectionate, fatherly expression, "The way I hear it is a bit different, son."

In fact, maybe I acknowledged that my father was right when I recorded those works: I thought of his "way" and gave them a bit more edge. But the first time, in Florence, I wanted to give them an aristocratic air.

*

After Vlad's departure in 1973 I learned that, for political reasons, his successor was to be a certain member of a given party. It was what we'd now call a politically motivated "apportioning." It bothered me deeply, because I feel that in some places the importance of cultural vision should prevail over that of political divides. The idea that whoever was nominated creative director would have to pick someone from the opposite party as the theater director, just to even the scales, embarrassed me as a musician. I had no say in the matter—the principal conductor doesn't decide things like that—but I couldn't see keeping quiet and not condemning such a procedure. So I let it be known that, if that's how the nomination was to be carried out, I would resign. The nomination was made, of course (I don't question the nominee's qualifications, so I don't intend to name him here), and I was limited to fighting the "rules."

This created a bit of a fuss. The orchestra interrupted its rehearsal with another conductor and mounted a strike on my behalf, and so did the chorus and ballet company and some of the technicians. The theater went through a period of crisis, complete with outside demonstrations and dissent among the internal factions, which wasn't without its spirited and humorous moments. Once, I was told, someone heatedly concluded, "Muti said so!"[15] to which someone else replied by citing the folk song "La leggenda del Piave": "Muti passaron quella notte i fanti, / tacere bisognava e andare avanti."[16] In any case, the person nominated never ended up taking the position. After a while everyone reconciled their differences, and Mario Polifroni became administrator. He was very open, and helped produce one of that period's best Maggio Musicale festivals.

We chose Spontini's *Agnes von Hohenstaufen*, which I had already done in 1970 at the RAI auditorium in Rome, upon Siciliani's invitation. Siciliani's shrewdness was much like the clever ploy Vlad had used to get me to do *L'Africaine*. One night when we met for dinner at his place he'd put the score on the piano and asked me to play the best parts—first and foremost (and it was no coincidence) the scene with the French knights from the sublime second act, when the orchestra plays the endless note Fedele D'Amico's review discussed in such fascinating words.[17] When I finished, Siciliani proclaimed in his characteristically good-humored, peremptory tone: "Muti, my dear, this is the opera for you; you *must* do it!" He was right, and I hope that before I leave this world I'll have the chance to perform *Agnes* in German, as Vienna and Berlin have requested.

The cast that time was stellar: Montserrat Caballé, Antonietta Stella, Giangiacomo Guelfi, Sesto Bruscantini, Bruno Prevedi. Montserrat was divine, even if, when the maestro first invited her to sing the part, she asked, "Maestro, what is *Agnes*, is it an opera?" In a passage that later became famous, the wind section imitates the sound of an organ. (Why don't they show that to students in conservatory composition classes on a daily basis?) At the end of the evening D'Amico himself came to my dressing room and literally pounced on the score as if to glean its secrets with his own eyes. And it's worth mentioning that the instrumentation was always that effective, even if in *Agnes von Hohenstaufen*—and perhaps in Spontini's work in general—the instrumentals are almost always hefty, what the Germans term *voller Satz* (full phrase, full score). On that historic occasion, still serenely smoking his cigarette, Siciliani whispered into my ear, "You know, Muti, Gui conducted it with the score!" When I met the elderly maestro in Florence and asked him why, he replied, "What do you expect? They all play together anyway, it's all the same!"

All this was during Polifroni's administration. You'll think it strange—and I don't mean to imply that, in order to do things well, theaters should replace their elected leadership with an appointed leadership!—but it all went well thanks to his honest foresight, in spite of the fact that he was burdened by the often unpopular task of overseeing everything. Mentality is what counts.

That run of *Agnes* brought about another important encounter when I met Corrado Cagli, the set and costume designer. Enriquez had shown me the fire-red volcanoes that Cagli—such a taciturn, grumpy, yet fascinating character—had in mind, and I was immediately taken by them. The cast was led by Leyla Gencer and Veriano Luchetti; Ms. Gencer once again, despite being somewhat older, did a marvelous rendition of Agnes.

*

In 1974, planning Verdi's *Macbeth* for the following year, I again called on Leyla Gencer, a great singer and dear friend of mine. The opera was in her repertoire, and I cast Mario Petri at her side, which some found an odd choice because he'd spent a few years working in film and making pop music. Contrary to the purists' predictions, he was an excellent Macbeth, played with real intelligence and stage presence. Paradoxically, the fact that his voice was no longer that of fifteen years earlier, and therefore wasn't as broad and robust in the aria "Pietà, rispetto, amore" in the last act, gave him the chance to more fully realize the author's dramatic intentions. Not only that, it helped him hit the particular tones, such as the parts whispered pianissimo, that were ultimately the ones Verdi had in mind—as I was happy to read in D'Amico's long profile of the baritone in his glowing review of the performance.[18] Verdi himself had rejected the idea of using a soprano because the voice would be too beautiful, and this piece called for something far from the usual bel canto, something with an expressionistic bent like the one that shines through in the long interview of Marianna Barbieri-Nini, the soprano who created the role of Lady Macbeth, assigning the voice a thousand different "expressions."

In the reading of the letter during the first act, for example, what should the orchestra's vaporized sound be if not fog? But with regard to this scene I should clarify that the jokes I exchanged with Gencer became, alas, a dialogue of the deaf, and it went on for days during the rehearsals: I'd ask to hear her "reading" and she'd reply that such things were to be done either on stage or not at all. Basically, she kindly, sweetly, and in a most feminine way refused to let me hear "Nel dì della vittoria io l'incontrai, stupito io n'era per le udite cose."[19]

My only option was to retreat and recommend she at least respect what was written for that measure: "You have to recite those lines," I said, "only so the audience understands. In reality, and in all likelihood, this is—as it would be if you were to read something with no one else around—read silently. You speak only because the audience has to know what's going on; if they can just barely hear you, that's enough." In practice, she should have no more than whispered over the orchestra's impalpably soft "carpet" of sound. I repeated my nice little explanation up until the day we came to that fatal moment during the first full rehearsal: the scene was set, and she could and would finally read. We began. Now, picture someone holding a megaphone to their mouth and shouting "NEL DÌ DELLA VITTORIA IO L'INCONTRAI," and she went on like that until the final "ADDIO," whose sheer power I've never forgotten! As happens in such cases, after all that fine work in the spoken sections, the sonorous attack that was supposed to be *sung*, "Ambizioso spirito tu sei Macbetto . . ."—and, yes, it called for a real voice—paled in comparison and seemed modeled on the most delicate anticlimax. So I understood why she hadn't wanted me to hear it beforehand. We tried to find some middle ground, and finally reached a compromise.

*

In 1976 Gluck's *Orfeo ed Euridice*, directed by Luca Ronconi and with sets by Pizzi, was a literal turning point for me. I had received a lot of praise up until then for my supposed "sanguine southernness" and therefore innate connection to Verdi, but these ideas are all theories and as such are rather stupid, as if it's somehow inevitable that someone from the South has Vesuvius in his veins. So there was a fair amount of anticipation, fueled also by the director, who was considered modern if not downright avant-garde at the time. We had great success, and to this day I consider that piece one of the best operas Ronconi has directed. (Some found it odd to see us "paired up so often,"[20] but I'm convinced that our long collaboration has been among the happiest.) The following year, however, Verdi's *Nabucco* created a few difficulties with the audience, thanks once again to Ronconi's direction. It was an incredibly popular opera, done here with a very modern staging that was set partially in the period of its composition—around the time of the Italian unification. Toward the end, to a good deal of sword brandishing, the king sang "Cadran, cadranno i perfidi" (They'll fall, the wicked shall fall) costumed according to the classic image of King Victor Emanuel II of Savoy. A few people were shocked, and when, fifteen minutes later, we appeared onstage to take a bow, I remember hearing someone shout, "Toss Ronconi into the Arno!" Indeed, the implications of the *Nabucco*-Savoy juxtaposition weren't entirely clear from the plot. In Verdi's opera, as in all melodrama, the good guys and the bad guys are separated like sheep from goats on Judgment Day, and the villain's sudden appearance *inter oves* (among the sheep)—setting the enemy among the chosen ones—was in fact quite ambiguous. On the whole, though, the direction was pure genius. The chorus, in nineteenth-century costumes and envisioned as the period audience of the opera's debut, sang from platforms by the stage above the orchestra, thereby resolving one of lyric theater's age-old directorial problems: where to put the chorus, and what to have them do. The backdrops were a series of large paintings done in the style of Francesco Hayez, perfectly realizing the concept of the tableau, those moments of immobile astonishment so present in genre melodramas, which in nineteenth-century Italian were referred to as *quadri*, "pictures" or even "paintings." The climax came at the emotional core of the opera, with the aria "Va', pensiero." The set featured, in addition to its painted backdrop, a field with harvesters frozen in the midst of gathering the wheat, their arms clasping the sheaves, lit from behind like silhouettes, almost as if they were actual statues, in a tableau that could have been titled *Belle statuine* (Beautiful Little Statues). It was fantastic! I've never seen a better set for that famous chorus. The scene when Abigaille unexpectedly steps out of another painting was equally excellent. I shared none of the audience's doubts, and considered that collaboration a prime example of the relationship that, by bringing the maestro and the *metteur en scène* together, propels a work toward the pinnacle of artistic expression.

*

I first performed Mozart in Florence in 1979, with *The Marriage of Figaro*. Luciano Alberti suggested I work with one of the most charismatic theatrical historians, Antoine Vitez, as director, and I'm proud to say that I was the first to bring him to Italy to work in an opera house. Helen Donath made a marvelous Susanna, and the production was a masterpiece. You can take me at my word, because a few years later I had the good fortune of doing the same opera at La Scala, with Giorgio Strehler directing. I'm grateful to Alberti for his idea: Vitez's direction held up perfectly when compared to Strehler's, and through his work France gave a real gift to Italy. And once again, the curiosity that roused public interest lay partially in people's desire to see how I, a "Verdian" conductor, would execute Mozart's opera.

In 1980, while still in Florence, I conducted my first *Otello*, with sets by Enrico Job and directed by the great Hungarian film director Miklós Jancsó. His contribution caused a bit of an uproar. At the end of the first act, for example, for the lovers' duet he'd envisioned a beautiful black woman walking partway across the stage, so she was seen between the arches along the side of the stage, holding a candle. The newspapers wrote about it with such exaggerated emphasis before opening night that this part—essentially a detail—threatened to overshadow the rest, so Jancsó was forced to cut the scene. He also had Otello use the prow of his ship to invade the bride's bed, which became another greatly discussed detail. (That performance marked Renato Bruson's debut as Iago, a character he "built" over the course of a month of practice at the piano with me.)

Toward the end of my time in Florence, in 1981, I did Gluck's *Iphigénie en Tauride*, directed by Sandro Sequi with sets by Giacomo Manzù. The sets were really beautiful, and I felt great reverence for Manzù. When I met him at a table at the Excelsior I immediately understood he cared little about social graces. He asked me to tell him the plot. As I did, also hinting at some of Gluck's musical solutions, he grabbed a sheet of paper and sketched out—somewhat distractedly, it seemed—a drawing that became the core of the enormous gold medallion that filled the set's background. So my story had inspired him to sketch out the set design, and that medallion was a few years ahead of its time; later, other stage directors caught on to the trend of immediately connecting with the audience through the use of a highly visible "object-symbol" capable of clarifying the director's idea of the opera, as if to more quickly convey his artistic intent. With *Ifigenia* Manzù was a precursor of sorts. Such experiences are rare, and happen only if you find yourself working with a genius. The wall was pink, and a lone chair was on the stage. That's another of Manzù's signatures; I was so enamored of it and of his work that many years later, when I conducted Verdi's *Macbeth* in Naples, I again asked him to do the set.

But by 1982 I knew my Florentine period had to come to a close, because I had three simultaneous posts conducting in Florence, London, and Philadelphia.

*

My relationship with London goes back to 1972, when the Philharmonia invited me to do a concert: it was my debut there, and was also the first time I conducted an English ensemble. The Philharmonia Orchestra was founded in 1945 by Walter Legge, a major recording manager, who'd gathered exceptional virtuosos who'd played under maestros like Karajan and Klemperer. It was Klemperer who brought the group back together after Legge's departure. They then took the name New Philharmonia, and that's what I conducted.

Orchestra musicians' lives were much less comfortable in England than in Italy. There were a lot of orchestras but essentially one hall, the Royal Festival Hall, and for lack of a stable space the musicians had to practice in schools, churches, or elsewhere, often moving from one to another on the same day, which entailed substantial difficulties. Sometimes they'd have three rehearsals in three different places. Because the rule at the time was "no play, no pay," managers aimed to secure the most work possible for their ensembles. An idle orchestra meant missed earnings, like an airplane grounded on the tarmac.

So their lives were exhausting, yet their patience was most admirable and the quality of their playing remained remarkably high. A few years later they turned an old building into their rehearsal space, calling it Henry Wood Hall, and their situation improved. They usually recorded at Abbey Road, the studio made famous by the Beatles. Adrian Boult, Thomas Beecham, and Edward Elgar had all recorded there.

At the Royal Festival Hall I conducted Brahms's Second Piano Concerto, followed by Mussorgsky's *Pictures at an Exhibition*. At the end of the rehearsals the musicians asked me if I'd like to stay on as their principal conductor. I was thirty-one and still had only intermittent contact with foreign orchestras; my relationship with the Wiener Philharmoniker, for instance, was limited to our 1971 performance of Donizetti's *Don Pasquale* in Salzburg, and I'd never been to America or worked with the Berliner Philharmoniker. So I was surprised and a bit puzzled that musicians who'd worked with Klemperer and Karajan would consider me, and I took some time to think it over—also because my spoken English was limited to what I'd learned in school, and London was a major musical capital.

In the end, what convinced me was essentially a repeat of what had happened in Florence: the idea came directly from the orchestra itself. And so I accepted a tenure destined to last ten years, from 1972 to 1982. I had a great relationship with the orchestra, and they ultimately made me conductor laureate. Alongside the joyous periods, my time there also had its fair share of sacrifices and bitter disappointments. But I met people who were quite important to me, including Sir Arnold (later Lord) Weinstock, former managing director of the General Electric Company, a real music lover and a good friend of the queen.

Over the course of the seventies, the orchestra began to win back its audience and regained its former glory in terms of musical quality. It began recording intensely—of my personal recordings catalogue, the Philharmonia did most of the EMI releases—and was soon considered the best English orchestra. We toured repeatedly, and the members decided to return to their old name, the one they'd had under Toscanini when they recorded Brahms's four symphonies: just "Philharmonia," shedding the "New." My role as principal conductor expanded when the orchestra nominated me music director.

One evening I was to conduct a concert in honor of Prince Charles, an amateur cellist and longtime orchestra patron; I left home on time but without my tailcoat. Nowadays a lot of conductors don't don tails, but it was unthinkable to perform before His Royal Highness without them. Lord Weinstock, a friend of the prince, sent him a message requesting that he arrive a little later so I'd have time to have someone pick up my coat.

We performed Prokofiev's *Alexander Nevsky* with Irina Archipova. Not only was she a great singer, but she was also a powerful woman in the Soviet Union, mingling with the elite group known as the nomenklatura. This was just as an international movement was rising in support of the dissident Anatoly Shcharansky, so when the mezzo-soprano's aria arrived and Irina rose to sing, a man jumped from the audience onto the platform and shouted, "Free Shcharansky!" I stopped, the police came, and we resumed, but then someone else jumped up yelling. We started over three times, and three times we were interrupted. Irina was quite shaken, but it all turned out fine. For me, it was incredibly annoying—it felt like they were committing an act of violence against the music, even though I do understand the exasperation that gave rise to those shouts. In the name of freedom they blocked the music, a key symbol of freedom.

*

Naturally, over the course of a long career not everything always goes so well. In 1973 I was to conduct *Il Trovatore* at the Paris Opéra, run by Rolf Liebermann, while the Solti-Strehler duo was engaged to produce Mozart's *Marriage of Figaro* in Versailles. It promised to be an excellent season, but then it all went wrong. The blame lay with the director. Liebermann had originally called on the legendary Luchino Visconti, but then Visconti fell gravely ill. Without being consulted, I was saddled with another director, who came up with an entirely new staging, a plan I wasn't fond of, and who decided to combine *Le Trouvère* and *Il Trovatore*—that is, to mix the French and Italian versions. I found that completely unacceptable, not to mention how strange it was that a director made a decision with such influence on the music, relegating me to the role of merely overseeing the soundtrack for the show. That happens a lot now, and it's due to directors' willingness to play fast and loose with certain details. From the very start, directors should lay the theatrical foundations of an opera through the music; I'd even venture that there is a process of musical direction entirely independent of theatrical direction. As if that weren't enough, this particular director wanted to use the finale of the French version, back-translated into Italian so it would be in keeping with the rest. I couldn't tolerate that idea, and staunchly opposed it. At the time, the charismatic Liebermann enjoyed a privileged position of unquestionable power within the European theatrical community. When I went to his office to express my consternation, he with his white mane, seated behind his almost Napoleonic desk, replied, "You are too young, Muti, to just up and leave *l'Opéra!*" I turned, left the room, and ran to catch a train for Italy.

*

The relationship between conductor and director is inevitably delicate. A few times I've had real difficulties. One of the better-known instances was at the 1992 Salzburg Festival, the first one Gérard Mortier managed, when I was to conduct *La clemenza di Tito* with the directorial couple Karl-Ernst and Ursel Herrmann. I completely agreed with them on the set design and overall structure, but their directorial oversight was careless when it came to the notes, and put the entire relationship between action and music into a state of crisis. At a certain point the mezzo in the role of Sesto was forced to sing her aria from the background, while the soprano playing Vitellia was in front of her performing a pantomime that had nothing to do with what Sesto was singing; it isolated Sesto from the orchestra, the conductor, and the audience.

Decisions of that sort expose a director's fundamental lack of trust in the power of music, as if the music is insignificant and insufficient without any action on stage, without something— anything—taking place. This is becoming a widespread bias: singers' performances are now accompanied by staged actions, giving the whole thing the feel of pantomime more than of oper- atic melodrama, as if there's some deep-seated disbelief in the idea that performers can effectively reach the audience solely through their use of the notes. This seems particularly unfounded in an opera like *La Clemenza di Tito*, where the aria, far from lacking action, condenses and sublimates all the action up to that point, and ends up going from an apparently anti-dramatic force to an evocatively super-dramatic one—as the most enlightened music historians have known for a few decades already. It's truly foolish to connect "drama" solely with brute action: those who do unwittingly fall victim to the term's etymology (the Greek *dr o*, "I do," "I act," "I make," indicates action). The Herrmanns had but one imperative: the performers always had to be doing something. We weren't able to reach a compromise, so I had to go.

Some criticized my decision, but to this day I'm convinced I did the right thing—although I'm not so irrational as to believe that, up on the podium, I need to agree with everything the director does. There were even times when I didn't really agree with all the ideas of a director I myself had chosen. For example, I loved Graham Vick and in 2001 I invited him to Salzburg for Mozart's *Magic Flute*, but I ended up not liking the production at all. In 2006 the festival managers jettisoned his staging and called Pierre Audi in to direct; his version was a success, since there were none of the provocative and mischievously offensive aspects that Vick's staging had had—things that became particularly problematic in an opera that was already enigmatic enough on its own. We all make some compromises, even if Votto would have preferred otherwise. What's important is that they don't become a form of prostitution.

There are many other directors I'd have liked to work with but never did. I met the great Ingmar Bergman after a concert in Stockholm with the Filarmonica della Scala. He was exceptionally knowledgeable about music, and had such sensitivity that he could formulate solid remarks about a piece he'd just heard, something like a real analysis. I asked him if we might do an opera together, but he confessed that—as soon as he completed his last film—he would be moving to an island. It's such a shame he never directed an opera!

The same thing happened with Federico Fellini. Naturally Nino Rota, who was Federico's favorite soundtrack composer, put us in touch. "No, dear maestro," he told me, "because sung words don't tell me much, since, unlike spoken words, they're completely beyond my control." Ditto with Bernardo Bertolucci, which I really regret, because I imagine he'd have been perfect for melodrama, given that he grew up in Emilia and directed the film *La Luna*—where he even used a piece from my recording of *Un ballo in maschera.*

When I invited Carmelo Bene, whom I considered a genius—and I knew he was a real opera lover—we planned to do *Il Trovatore* or *Macbeth*, but he requested so many rehearsals that we simply couldn't fit it into the theater's calendar. That really disappointed me, because I have a vivid recollection of my reaction to one of his performances. He began reciting, and within two minutes his voice had absorbed me to the point where I was completely lost. It was so enchanting, you couldn't help but feel one with it, giving yourself up in order to delve into the sheer experience of that sound.

All these artists could have made an extraordinary contribution to Italian opera, and would have complemented my enthusiastic collaborations with such excellent directors as Robert Carsen, Vick, and Jancsó.

CHAPTER FIVE

L'orchestra del destino

As a conductor, Karajan was always open to newer generations; he spotted many talents, and—whatever may be said about him and his motives, which some believe weren't always strictly aesthetic— all contemporary conductors over fifty owe him recognition. His status as an artist is beyond question. He invented a new orchestral sound, a musical phrasing and elegance that, at the time, sounded like nothing ever heard before. Back then, the opposite trend seemed predominant; in music schools "objectivity" was championed, and pushed to the point of preemptive complacency. On the one hand there was Karajan, on the other the schools—that's how it was. It seems to me that's pure fact, and I don't care to hazard a cursory judgment that others are better equipped to give than I.

Karajan knew of my work and its results, and in 1971 he invited me to Salzburg to conduct *Don Pasquale*. Since then I've been at every festival but one for the past forty years, and on August 24, 2010, I received a special medal commemorating my 200th appearance on that podium. I've conducted *Don Giovanni*, *Così fan tutte*, *La Traviata*, *The Magic Flute*, *La Clemenza di Tito*, *Otello*, *Moïse*, and *Orfeo*.

I first met the Wiener Philharmoniker in May 1971 in Vienna, at the Sophiensaal, for the rehearsals of *Don Pasquale*, which laid the foundation for our work together that July. That hall was often used for recording their albums as well.

I was a bit scared, and on top of that I got there late, with my heart in my mouth (that never happens to me). A few musicians were outside smoking, and I began to worry that my relationship with the ensemble would end before it had even begun. As we began the rehearsals, I looked all around. I was surrounded by a bunch of older musicians who still remembered maestros like Wilhelm Furtwängler, Bruno Walter, Hans Knappertsbusch, Josef Krips, and Ferenc Fricsay from the early postwar period. Some of them had even played *The Magic Flute* with Toscanini in Salzburg. This was the orchestra of the major conductors who'd come from the theaters of the Hapsburg Empire—and there I was, with the heavy hitters!

They dressed as everyone did in old Vienna, a city whose air was still reminiscent of the Eastern Bloc. What I mean is that, in 1971, if you looked at how the locals dressed, the difference between Vienna and Budapest wasn't that big. Basically, it was a drab, dreary city.

Similarly, the musical climate was solemn enough to make a real impression on someone like me, a young man from Italy. You were almost afraid you'd run into Beethoven and Haydn on the street, or that you'd find Brahms and Bruckner and Schönberg on the Musikverein's grand staircase. Everything was somehow stuffy and weighty. Luckily for me, I could turn to Donizetti for help: we spoke the same language.

And so we began. The ease with which the strings sang out was entirely new to me, and tangibly different from the Italian mode that had developed in opera and even in Donizetti's repertoire over the years; yet it had something deep and dark that, without having the Italians' luster, nevertheless gave the impression it got closer to the soul of the notes. I don't mean to say they understood that music better than Italians, but I must admit that, with their manner of playing, I did get the feeling their roots ran somewhat deeper. It was *Don Pasquale*, it wasn't Beethoven's Seventh, and yet, in the way they played Donizetti, you caught glimpses of a symphonic tradition that, as I've said—was somehow inaccessible to Italians ever since they'd exclusively decided to give music a lighter "lilt." It might also be true that this was the Italians' way of staying closer to Donizetti's original style and world, but that morning in the Sophiensaal I suddenly discovered an orchestra capable of getting at the heart of an 1843 *dramma buffo* (tragicomedy) without severing the ties that linked it to Haydn, Beethoven, Schumann, and Brahms. A distant world stood before me, and I found it both disturbing and intriguing. It was a miracle: it was like raising the veil covering a mysterious monument on the day of its inauguration.

My experience listening to albums was, of course, something else entirely. Until that day, only albums had been capable of conveying something of that sound. Here, I gestured and a sound arose, a musical element that only partially corresponded to what I'd asked for: it was the musicians offering me their entire, very rich history. I looked at them in their black jackets, the most superficial sign of a world I can only describe, for lack of a better word, as "ancient." The ensemble was identical to the one used for the same type of opera in Italian theaters, but here the sound was fuller.

Consider, for example, the attack, the first measures. All hell broke loose, and I had to explain at some length that Donizetti is a bit different from Verdi in his *Otello* period. To make sure they got it, I suggested they imagine a sound more akin to Mozart. The difference in "sound" between various composers—especially composers of different eras—is something conductors should pay more attention to. Oftentimes, even with the most serious works by Rossini, I hear something practically indistinguishable from Verdi, in both the strings and brasses, and it doesn't take an advanced degree in music to understand that that's absurd.

My communication with the musicians was aided by my singing the various passages (I enjoy that, and always do it). Often they immediately understood, based on the way I sang, certain nuances and details of phrasing without any wordy explanations. And the sound changed according to how I'd sung. That was all they needed because, obviously, they knew the opera inside out. Don't forget that the program, on successive evenings, often ranged from *Wozzeck* to the *Barber of Seville*, *Parsifal*, *Don Carlos*, and *La forza del destino*.

*

My relationship with the Wiener Philharmoniker lasted over the years, and we reached a particular harmony with the work of Mozart—I did my first *Jupiter* with them, and also his Symphony in G Minor, K. 550; just imagine how scared I was at the idea of facing its utterly unique beginning!—then moved on to Brahms and Schubert. They requested that program, evidently viewing me as a bridge of sorts between two musical cultures, German-Austrian and Italian. Schubert was enormously influenced by

Italian music, beginning with Rossini. More or less everyone agrees on that, but it seems most are afraid to openly say so, since the commonly held belief that Italians are provincial makes it hard for many to admit that Schubert, the Austrian giant, took something from the Swan of Pesaro. And the Wiener Philharmoniker loved the combination of these two distinct musical traditions that our collaboration created. I drew from that stylistic source for decades, because the sound is closer than others to my ideal: in some respects they can even be violent (if Stravinsky's *Rite of Spring* is on their stands), while in other respects they never lose their ideal *velluto*, their velvety sound. This characteristic goes back all the way to the beginning of their symphonic work, covering a long and historically uninterrupted path.

*

In 1982 I conducted Mozart's *Così fan tutte*. Here's how it went: During a U.S. tour with the Philharmonia Orchestra of London, playing in Boston, New York, and Chicago, I ended up in Raleigh, North Carolina. I was staying at a motel—one of those beehive-like places that are so common in America, with balconies and outdoor staircases—when, at seven o'clock one morning, the phone rang and a firm, straightforward voice said: "It's Karajan."

"There's a crazy guy on the line who wants to joke around," I said to Cristina.

The voice asked: "Have you ever conducted *Così fan tutte*?"

I began to think it actually could be Karajan, and decided to humor him: "No, maestro. But right now Karl Böhm is doing it in Salzburg, with great success. I wouldn't want to die by my own baton. Can I think it over?"

"I don't have time for that: it's yes or no."

"If it's really you asking, I accept."

"Don't mention this to anyone. The advisory board has differing opinions, and I'll bring up your name at the opportune time."

Things went the way fate would have it—the right way. The critics, like *prefiche*,[1] had already begun to bristle at the idea, snickering: "Bravo Muti, conducting *Così fan tutte*, thus committing professional suicide."[2]

But my rendition got rave reviews in the German-language press. Perhaps the secret lay, to some extent, in the fact that my approach was antithetical to their tradition, which focuses on the music, making the notes envelop the lyrics. I, on the contrary, took Lorenzo Da Ponte's libretto as my point of departure, and from his words arrived at Mozart's music. The result was quite different from anything they were canonically accustomed to. Even the musicians themselves went from cautious curiosity to open enthusiasm. The staging was directed by Michael Hampe, and the sets, by Mauro Pagano, were absolutely fantastic, as were the costumes. Each evening, as the boat arrived during the second act, the crowd audibly gasped in wonder.

Then one day, entirely by chance, I discovered why that opera was set in Naples even though the libretto mentions the city only once. I had wondered about that for a long time, until one morning in Vienna I ran into a very elderly musicologist in front of Saint Stephen's Cathedral. After he congratulated me, his voice took on the tone of a subversive revolutionary, and he leaned closer to my ear to tell me that the story really had taken place in Wiener Neustadt (*neue Stadt*, "new city" in German) but, out of discretion, the location had been transliterated as Naples (*Nea-polis*, "new city" in Greek).

That production was performed several years in a row, from 1982 to 1988, and Karajan—a staunch supporter after seeing me conduct *Don Giovanni*—invited me back to the festival again the following year. Just think: one day I conducted that opera right after doing a dress rehearsal of *Così fan tutte* the same morning!

*

My collaboration with the Wiener Philharmoniker has perhaps been the most important one of my entire life. It began in 1971 and today, as I write this, it's still going strong. It's covered all the years I've worked at Salzburg, and even in the one year I didn't participate in the festival, I nevertheless performed with them elsewhere.

I recorded all of Schubert's symphonies with them, and afterward they invited me to conduct their 1993 New Year's concert. I didn't feel I had a real handle on the sublime Viennese tradition of *Unterhaltungsmusik*,[3] so I was hesitant. They replied that Schubert—whom I conducted quite well, they felt—was the gateway to Strauss, so I had no excuses. I did such performances with them more than once, but stopped after a while because, in that type of concert, the repetition—the ceremoniousness, the spectacle, the whole thing—can end up extinguishing one's creative drive.

One of our most important performances was of Haydn's *Die Schöpfung* (The Creation), which I was doing for the first time. In 1995 I conducted a concert celebrating the 125th anniversary of the Musikverein, following the exact same program with which they'd made their debut (it was incredibly long, as most century-old programs were). They often invited me to mark such events. Ater the 125th anniversary in 1995,

in 1996 Austria celebrated its millennial year, so we played in
the Hofmusikkapelle, the country's oldest musical institution,
founded by Maximilian I in 1498, and in 1997 we played on the
850th anniversary of Saint Stephen's Cathedral. The crown-
ing event of all those performances came in 1992 when, during
the concert celebrating the orchestra's 150th anniversary, I was
awarded the Philharmonic Gold Ring, which implies a mystical
marriage of sorts with that venerable institution. Later, in 2001,
I received the Nicolai Medal, named for its founder and first conductor, Otto Nicolai.

*

Austria therefore became my second home, not only from a
musical point of view but in a more personal sense, because I
also participated in the Staatsoper–Theater an der Wien productions. Our first together was *Aida* in 1973—my compatriots
Paolo Grassi and Massimo Bogianckino were also there!—followed two years later by my first tour with them, in which I conducted several concerts after Karl Böhm had stepped down.

I performed with the Wiener Philharmoniker many times
in Italy, and more than once in Naples.

And the orchestra stayed right by my side even through
rough times, like my departure from La Scala. I did a concert
there with them, scheduled long before, just a month after my
resignation on May 2, 2005. Everyone knew, and felt, that it was
an emotional evening. The ensemble really came together—
around me, with me, and for me. That was the last time I conducted at La Scala. I feel it's only right that I call them the
orchestra I was destined for—"l'orchestra del destino."[4]

CHAPTER SIX

Music for the New World

I started my collaboration with the Philadelphia Orchestra while I was still in London. It began by pure coincidence, as I'd never performed in the United States, I had no powerful manager or big record company backing me, nor had EMI ever tried to condition my decisions with an eye on my "career" (that terrible word).

In 1971 I was director of the Maggio Musicale Fiorentino festival and I was rehearsing Beethoven's oratorio *Christus am Ölberge* (Christ on the Mount of Olives). My rehearsal ended at one. The Philadelphia Orchestra was in town with Eugene Ormandy, and like all serious conductors he got to the theater well before his rehearsal was scheduled to begin. He asked who I was, they told him about me, and he sat at the back of the auditorium, partially hidden by the red velvet curtains, and listened to me for a half hour. At his concert I sat next to Vittorio Gui, and Ormandy conducted Beethoven's Seventh. My esteemed companion was one of those taciturn, impenetrable men who can say it all with an eyebrow, and I noticed something that evening, a tinge of irony in the air, so I asked him. He replied dryly, "So, the Seventh calls for four trumpets, who knew?" At the time there was a tendency to double the winds in order to balance out the strings, but tweaking the brasses—a practice begun by Wagner for the Ninth—was the riskiest thing you could do, and that evening there were indeed four trumpets.

At the sumptuous reception afterward—the American consulate was right near City Hall—not only did Gui look rather vexed, but even Farulli had a prim and uncertain bearing. I didn't understand where their harsh criticism was coming from. I had been amazed by the orchestra's precision, intonation, participation, and discipline. Their entrances were perfect, something I hadn't experienced before. The strings, for example, all had the same *spiccato*, the same *balzato*, and when they were supposed to be using the upper half of the bow, you could rest assured not one was out of position. In short, they displayed a downright mathematical symmetry. Because I was fascinated, as a conductor myself, by this technical ability, and dazzled by such unheard-of virtuosity, I hadn't even posed the question of "interpretation."

The following day I had lunch with Ormandy at Patricia Volterra's splendid home in Bellosguardo. (She had been the wife of an important pianist whose career was compromised by the racial laws and ultimately interrupted by World War II; when he returned to Italy after the war, he made his name as an art expert, which he'd always been. Patricia became such a close friend that she was godmother to my firstborn son, Francesco, just as Gui's wife Elda was for Domenico, and the Count and Countess Guidi, who lived across from me in the Palazzo Ginori, for Chiara.) Ormandy said he was quite impressed by the half-hour rehearsal he'd heard, and he invited me to debut in America in 1972. The program of the October 27 concert included, among other works, Mozart's Symphony in C, K. 338, a solo concerto, and Prokofiev's Third Symphony. The orchestra was astonished, and Norman Carol, the charismatic first violin, came to my dressing room to inquire why an elegant conductor like me, after doing Mozart, would then perform music as violent and aggressive as Prokofiev's.

I performed the same concert at Carnegie Hall in New York, and the legendary Harold C. Schonberg introduced me in the pages of the *New York Times* with an article titled "Riccardo Muti: Master of Baton." Over the next few years I was invited back for longer stays, and Daniel Webster, music critic for the *Enquirer*, wrote enthusiastic reviews. And so it was that in 1976, for the first time in his forty-year tenure in America, Ormandy decided to name a principal guest conductor, and chose me. I was happy to receive the honor, which foreshadowed my promotion to music director of the Philadelphia Orchestra four years later.

Actually, I was given that position in 1979, during an important period in my private life, as the birth of my third child, Domenico, approached. Like his siblings, he was born at the Donatello Clinic in Florence, under the care of Dr. Montanelli, the clinic's chief obstetrician. (Francesco was born right after the fourth performance of *L'Africaine*, on the morning of May 6, 1971, and Chiara on February 26, 1973, during my rehearsals for *La Traviata* in Paris.) They told me Domenico had been born, and I faced the dilemma of either dropping everything to go back to Florence (as a father should) or moving forward with the rehearsals we'd already begun and sparing them the task of finding a substitute (as a good maestro should). In the end I decided to stay, and consoled myself with the thought that, if I were captain of a ship circumnavigating the globe, I wouldn't have the luxury of hopping on a jet whenever I wished. But Cristina was alone, and that pained me. Leaving the kids so I could roam the world was always hard, even though I knew Cristina had everything under control and they all knew they were constantly in my thoughts. I remember that on my return from a long time away I'd just set my luggage down and go pick them up at school, and I can still picture their ecstatic expressions. Every once in a while I'm surprised when one of their drawings pops up between the sheets of my scores, where they'd hidden it for me.

When I got to the clinic I asked to see little Domenico, and as I looked at the newborns behind the glass I couldn't tell which one was him; I checked all twenty of them, twice, but felt no natural pull toward any of them. In the end that was all right: Domenico was out getting a test, so it was perfectly fine that I felt no emotional reaction to any of the twenty newborns sleeping behind the glass. He's named after my father and my great-grandfather who, after being single most of his life (a life, I've always been told, he led quite seriously, almost as a public figure), continued the family name when he decided to get married, at age seventy-seven, to a thirty-year-old named Beatrice. The Muti family had been in Molfetta since the early sixteenth century, and local records show some of them had worked as notaries.[1] Domenico Muti was a laborer and farmer, which must have given him a degree of strength and determination in the choices he made, like marrying so late in life.

*

In 1980 I was music director in Philadelphia, director of the Maggio Musicale festival in Florence, and conductor in London. It was a lot to handle, and looking back now I wonder how I managed it. I would inevitably have to leave at least one of those posts, and the first city I bid adieu was Florence. The decision had nothing to do with my degree of emotional attachment; I was tightly bound to that city, it's where my children were born and my friends lived. But maybe there was an art-related motive—I felt I'd somehow exhausted my possibilities after all those (often courageous) rehearsals, new attempts, and experiments.

The second city I had to leave was London, a choice determined by my acceptance of the offer to work as music director in America. That role is the top of the pyramid, and brings with it a series of decisions (to be made in consultation with management) as well as immense responsibility with regard to the life of the orchestra and its programs, its relationship to the city, tours, recording sessions—in short, everything. And that particular orchestra was, and certainly still is, a real "war machine," with an incredibly vast repertoire that—at least in terms of the works' technical demands—it could pick up and play immediately, virtually without rehearsing, which meant that my conducting had to match that. I obviously didn't have a hold on their entire repertoire yet, so I had to quickly bring myself up to speed.

Furthermore, one of my tasks was to include contemporary music in the program whenever possible, especially that of American composers. Those works were often written on commission, and were often so complex as to make Stravinsky's *Rite of Spring* look like a stroll in the park. Indeed, alas, the stylistic mark they all shared was—aside from an interest in color—an enormous rhythmic complexity that you had to pull from the orchestra without the slightest slip, or risk the piece falling apart. My relationship to contemporary music is a chapter unto itself, and in Italy virtually no one knows anything about it. There the critics, and with them the public, probably thought I wasn't very interested in contemporary music, which I can disprove by pointing to my work at La Scala, where I regularly conducted pieces by Salvatore Sciarrino, Luca Francesconi, Giacomo Manzoni, and Ivan Fedele, to name just a few.

*

Working with the Philadelphia Orchestra also meant I had to deepen my symphonic repertoire. We did Mahler's First, Scriabin's symphonies, and many others, almost all of which were recorded. Broadening the repertoire was right, useful, and ultimately unavoidable. One day I understood that better than ever when a first violin, catching me off guard, asked, "Maestro, why is it that you, an Italian, never do Respighi?" I immediately realized two things: on the one hand, I saw the scope of my ignorance (aside from his two or three most famous compositions I barely knew his work) and, on the other, how common it was for Italians to feel his work was best not performed. What was I guilty of? Maybe acquiescing to the fascist regime, insofar as I was an Italian academic—but in that sense my situation was a lot like that of Mascagni, Pirandello, and many others. It was a preconceived stance, and all of us students of Italian conservatories were at once both guilty and unaware of it. Our prejudice was not shared by the world's great orchestras, who unabashedly played those works—and not just the Roman trilogy but also his

Trittico botticelliano, his violin concertos, and so on. Toscanini and Karajan, for example, often conducted Respighi.

Faced with that question, I had to admit, tail tucked between my legs, that I didn't know his work very well. I began studying it and emphasize once again, knowingly, that even though Respighi didn't leave us a vast repertoire, his work is nevertheless interesting and deserves attention: his scores display the orchestration of true masterpieces. I then began to reflect on composers like Giovanni Sgambati, Giuseppe Martucci, and Ferruccio Busoni, who paid a hefty price for venturing away from melodrama, the only genre that was popular at the time and soon became all the rage. And yet Toscanini insisted that his programs include music by composers like Martucci, who is now all but forgotten and who, along with his peers, aimed to preserve the line of Italian music between the eighteenth and twentieth centuries. I should mention once again Gui's perspicacity; in a 1914 commemoration, he described Martucci as "a unique voice, isolated in the very country in which he grew up like an exotic plant . . . a country where, at the time, there was no form of musical expression except for theater, and theater was not necessarily always synonymous with—as it still is not today—art."[2]

I recorded Respighi's Roman trilogy as an album; when I proposed performing it at La Scala, where it hadn't been played for decades, a few slightly fundamentalist critics reproached me—exactly what happened in Florence with *Cavalleria rusticana* and *Pagliacci*. Today, of course, things have changed, and Respighi's melodramatic oeuvre is being reconsidered as well. I hope one day the same impulse will extend to the work of Giorgio Federico Ghedini, Ildebrando Pizzetti, Gian Francesco

Malipiero, and Franco Alfano, who not only were effective composers but also had admirable cultural concepts. (I had the good
fortune of meeting the first two in person, and can guarantee
their ideas were extraordinary.)

Unfortunately, that entire period has disappeared and will
have difficulty rising up again because, in the minds of those who
plan the symphonic season's programs—with the exception of
the indispensable and preponderant presence of the classics—it
risks coming into competition with contemporary Italian works.
It's certainly good that an effort is made to introduce the latter,
but I hope that, sooner or later, the dust will be wiped away and
our twentieth- and late-nineteenth-century symphonic works
will be brought back to the concert halls, much as the past few
years have seen a renewed interest in baroque repertoire and
performance praxis.

*

I recorded Beethoven's symphonies with the Philadelphia
Orchestra, and in America it was the first time they were recorded
on CD. I'm also proud that we did the same thing with the work
of Alexander Scriabin—the orchestra related exceptionally well
to his brilliant, fantastic instrumentation.

But of all the concerts, two deserve special mention. The
first was during Reagan's presidency, and the musicians wanted
to perform a concert against nuclear rearmament, an idea I
wholeheartedly agreed with. But for me, as an Italian, it was no
small decision. Those on the opposite side of public opinion—
which counts for a lot in America—basically told me I should
just go back home. Outside the theater two men wearing sand-
wich boards even protested *against* the concert.

The other event, which was televised, was the 1991 memorial concert for Martin Luther King, Jr., one of the most moving evenings of my entire career. I need to preface this by saying that the number of nonwhites in the audience at America's major musical institutions is usually quite low; most of the faces you see are of European descent, however recent or distant, and therefore most of the audience comes from, or at least has roots in, the Western cultural tradition. In a city like Philadelphia, when you climb to the podium and tell yourself you're making music for the public, for the "community," you should honestly ask yourself exactly what community that would be.

The overwhelming sensation, and conclusion, you'd then come to is that you're making music for the elite. An apt reference, by bitter antiphrasis, is the famous line from the Gospel according to Matthew: *Multi sunt vocati, pauci vero electi* (Many are called, few are chosen). The multiethnic makeup of American society and the serious sociocultural problems that still challenge its population are likely what cause the "community" to be a *communitas* only in an entirely abstract sense. I've experienced nothing of the sort in Europe or in Japan, because in Europe and Japan things are different.

In the concert for Martin Luther King, Jr., the chorus was made up entirely of people of color. The American basketball superstar Julius Erving (the legendary Dr. J) performed in Aaron Copland's *Lincoln Portrait*, and in the photo they took of us afterward the photographer caught me laughing: Erving and I looked like we were the same height, but only because he'd courteously kneeled! During the performance I turned around to see, for once, an audience that was 90 percent people of color. I'd been asked to precede the national anthem (and I knew this, but it was a surprise for the whites in the audience) with the so-called Black National Anthem, "Lift Every Voice and Sing," and everybody, whites included, jumped to their feet. It was a powerfully moving evening and for me, as I said, it was one of the strongest experiences of my entire life—not least because, beginning with the concert right after that, I knew the audience would go back to what it had always been, a white audience. It was a priceless experience, and in Erving, the super-tall star of the evening, the giant adored in every American stadium, I found a dedication equal to that of Tino Carraro on the Italian stage.

*

They had grown fond of me, just as they had in Florence, and if you happen to visit the Academy of Music and cross the street to see the old theater, which bears the names of everyone who made that theater a great institution—Leopold Stokowski, Eugene Ormandy, Mario Lanza, and many others—you'll see my name on the far right. That hall, made famous as millions of people watched Leopold Stokowski and the Philadelphia Orchestra play the soundtrack of Disney's *Fantasia*, had also had Toscanini on its podium. And to give you an idea of who its regulars were, I remember seeing a photograph in Ormandy's office with the maestro at the center, surrounded by three violinists—none other than Nathan Milstein, David Oistrakh, and Isaac Stern. In Italy, or anywhere else, for that matter, when we talk with a degree of haughtiness about "lightweight" America, we would do well to reflect on those musical giants.

The hall's only defect was its acoustics, a problem that arose from its "traditional" arrangement as an opera house.

(This happens a lot in Italy as well.) When you move the orchestra from the pit to the stage, especially without any corrective acoustic chambers, which weren't thought of at the time, the balance is lost and the conditions are clearly not the same as in Berlin's Philharmonie, Amsterdam's Concertgebouw, Vienna's Musikverein, or Moscow's Tchaikovsky Auditorium.

It worried me that such a large and historic city did not have an adequate concert hall, so that the traditional theater could be reserved for ballet and opera. I began a fundraising campaign of sorts. This met with some opposition at first: the traditionalists were reluctant to abandon the hall they affectionately referred to as the Grande Dame. I went on explaining that I wasn't driven by self-congratulatory motives—I didn't want a space just for me, founded by me—because sooner or later I'd be going back to Italy. Rather, I wanted to do it for them; after all, they were the ones who suffered when the symphonic rehearsal schedule overlapped with the opera rehearsal schedule, while the ballet was relegated to the in-between times.

Sell, the manager, immediately believed in the project, as did part of the board, and together we raised enough to build the exquisite Kimmel Center. The hall is just down the street from the Academy and, despite a few minor acoustic problems that need correcting, it is marvelous. The center's various spaces are named after various conductors, and they dedicated the library to me, so I'm proud to be a part of the institution's very heart.

*

I stayed in Philadelphia until 1992. I decided to perform my last concert as music director, twenty years after my debut with that orchestra, in Jerusalem, in recognition of the spirituality and syncretism that have characterized that city for more than two millennia. It was my farewell to the orchestra, and because I had chosen Martucci for the encore, they gave me a shirt with his name printed on the back; after my attack, they performed the rest of the *Notturno* all on their own.

CHAPTER SEVEN

At La Scala

O NCE again I had to leave, because I'd been offered the directorship of La Scala beginning in 1986. I had no choice but to resign from the Philadelphia Orchestra. An opera house demands infinite energy, and it would have been impossible to reconcile that with the complex responsibilities that working in America entailed, not to mention the demands of my relationships with ensembles in Vienna and Paris and the Bayerische Rundfunk in Munich. Meanwhile, the orchestra of La Scala seemed in need of rehabilitation—the musicians themselves had called on me for that very reason—which would take a long time and require intense commitment. I hesitated for a bit, and feared I'd feel nostalgia for Philadelphia, but then, in 1985 in London where I was rehearsing an opera, I signed the contract. At the end of the year I was already part of the hiring committee for new musicians.

That was the start of a long period that began with *Nabucco*, directed by Roberto De Simone. On December 7, 1986, at the opening of my first season at La Scala, the chorus's encore caused a stir, and I've always thought that this showed the major interest surrounding the world of opera in Italy, not only among opera enthusiasts but in the population at large. (There was even an interview about it with Craxi.)[1] The custom of concluding performances at La Scala with an encore had ended decades before, the night that Toscanini, to the audience's very vocal disappointment, forbade the lead tenor to do one after *Un ballo in maschera*. There was perhaps one exception to the unwritten moratorium when Gianandrea Gavazzeni conducted Verdi's *I Lombardi*, with "O Signor che dal tetto natio"), but the practice was virtually abolished.

The cast that evening was fantastic. Ghena Dimitrova played Abigaille, and everything went smoothly even though there was a degree of excitement in the air following Abbado's departure and my arrival. As the orchestral introduction led up to the chorus's entrance, I felt through my back a growing tension behind me; words can't explain it, because that kind of thing resides not in the conscious mind, but rather in the secret DNA every Italian shares. It was a combination of tension and expectation. The chorus, under Giulio Bertola's guidance, phrased everything with a uniquely Italian tone, proving—through a skill inherited from one generation to the next—they understood and could enunciate every word. I held the last note for a long time, and took the license of making it much longer than what's written: I wanted to show an "affectionate affinity" between lament and hope, a true personal yearning for light in the prisoner, who knows that the banks of the river Jordan are an illusion but nevertheless refuses to give up. When it ended there was a moment of silence, then massive applause, which must have been due in part to the excellent performance—I assure you I'm not boasting about it, as it was relatively unimportant to me—but was also largely an expression of thanks for having brought that particular work back to the people of Milan, as they could fully appreciate it only in that theater, *their* theater. La Scala had also housed the work's very first performance in 1853, so it was as if the Milanese had finally found something dear that they'd lost—an impression reinforced by the libretto and the aria "Va', pensiero," with the line "O mia patria sì bella e perduta" (Oh, my country, so beautiful and lost).

When I raised the baton to signal the start of Zaccaria's part, the audience began shouting, "Encore!" This happened thrice, and what I already knew then became patently clear: it wasn't a tribute to me, but to Verdi and his marvelous musical number. I knew full well, in theory, that I couldn't allow an encore. The ban was part of La Scala's unofficial code of conduct, which had given the theater its well-deserved status in the twenties, making it a model for opera houses worldwide; even the strict attention to time, which ensured that a performance scheduled for eight o'clock began right at eight, was the legacy of Toscanini's precision. Everything and everyone, from the maestro to the technicians, had to run like clockwork. With their third request I began wondering what to do. "If you don't do it," I said to myself, "you'll be letting thousands of people down; if you do it, you'll be violating a sacred tradition." I raised my head and looked at the chorus that De Simone had ranged on the proscenium, so serious and composed; in their eyes I saw a subtle yet clear sign: many of them were pushing me to do it. So I launched back into the introduction, accompanied by grateful applause, and we redid that number. It turned out perhaps even better than the first time around, although I reduced my gestures so I virtually wasn't conducting. It wasn't me, but rather Verdi, *Nabucco*,

"Va', pensiero," La Scala, Milanese pride, Italy. It was a magical moment with an undeniable dash of patriotism, especially in the sense of a solid identity, as if they were saying, "This is what we are." From there on out, the night was a triumph.

The morning after, the newspapers were all talking about it. Craxi, if I recall correctly, was against the encore. A do of that sort gives you an idea of what Italy can be like. It's heartbreaking to say so today, as the recent debate about legislation that has penalized the Italian music world is still so fresh.[2] At least in 1986 the love of melodrama that ran through our veins was so strong it sometimes erupted into such excessively exuberant outpourings. This makes it clear what a deep part of us music really is, and how it stays—as Frederick II would say—*nostris affixa medullis*, embedded in the marrow of our bones.

*

Of course I did many operas at La Scala, not only Mozart and Wagner but also Gluck, who was rarely played back then; I did five of his works. One evening in 1993, along with *Pagliacci*, I conducted Stravinsky's *Baiser de la fée*, although it generally isn't done by the music director, nor in an otherwise operatic evening. I wanted to prove what was already known—that ballet music is, more often than not, an excellent symphonic score that calls for (and many seem to ignore this fact) as much care as everything else in the repertoire. One must also consider that the choreography often has to start from the music, rather than absurdly reversing the hierarchy to privilege the choreography, as happens sometimes (and inevitably whenever there are flesh-and-blood dancers working with a recording instead of a live orchestra).

We did one of our rarer operas in 1991, Cherubini's *Lodoïska*, directed by Ronconi; then came Spontini, Pergolesi, Poulenc, and more Verdi. In 1987–88 I decided, with the understanding and help of general manager Carlo Maria Badini, to perform all three of Mozart's Italian operas in one month. It was a landmark aim for a theater that until then had simply been considered a "Verdian" theater.

Don Giovanni was directed by Strehler, the second time we'd worked together; the first was in 1981 on *The Marriage of Figaro*. At the beginning we were suspicious of one another, scrutinized one other, each well aware of his own temperament, and, you might say, checked each other out, both curious to see who'd be the first to act high-handedly. We knew our dispositions could either help us get along marvelously or launch us into battle. There are some photographs that illustrate, better than any other documentation, how it all went. Onstage at the beginning of rehearsals (he attended some of mine and I all of his, as should be the case with any staging you really respect) he sat stage left, I stage right, with a great void between us. One of us would make an observation, the other would make another. Without either of us noticing, little by little our seats began moving toward the center, so we found ourselves right next to one another—see lower photo on page 17 of the photo insert—as we showered the poor singers with instructions. The production, with Samuel Ramey singing Figaro, and sets by Enzo Frigerio, was an extraordinary success.

Two years later, in 1983, when I still didn't have a set position at La Scala, we performed *Ernani*, directed by Ronconi. Musically—and I've often listened to the recording—I still think it was well performed, but the staging was questionable, and a few details were definitely embarrassing. For example, the chorus was sunk into several hollows in the stage—this in a highly choral melodrama with intense choruses like the third act's "Si ridesti il leon di Castiglia"—which prevented the singers from establishing full contact with the audience, halting the opera's momentum and inhibiting its expressive possibilities. Some of them even joked about it: "We're *Ernani*'s all-dwarf chorus!" and "Here I am, they've turned me into a dwarf!"[3] They weren't so far off: you saw them only from the waist up. But if comments like that start circulating in public, they invariably hurt the production—which is precisely what happened, despite the fact that the show as a whole and all its accoutrements were a technical triumph of set design and staging. The critics ended up panning the whole thing, including a few of the more clever parts I still find undeniably beautiful.

*

I then began my long adventure as music director in 1986. Naturally, I performed a lot of Verdi, especially in the anniversary year of 2001.[4] The *Financial Times* considered La Scala's season the only one of all the world's theaters that offered a real contribution to a rereading of Italy's great opera composer. As for me, my aim has always been to bring Verdi back into his scores. In 1973, when I conducted *Aida* in Vienna, Hans Swarowsky wrote me, first and foremost, to praise my "fidelity"; that doesn't mean just doing what's written, but rather trying to capture the infinite possibilities that lie latent within the notation. You have to proceed, as Saint Paul says, *non atramento, sed spiritu.*[5] It is in that "spirit" that I took up the "popular" trilogy of *Rigoletto*, *Il Trovatore*, and *La Traviata*.

La Traviata, in 1990, caused quite a commotion. After it was scheduled, I was traveling the globe and no one could believe me when I said it hadn't been performed at La Scala for twenty-six years—since 1964, conducted by Karajan with Mirella Freni as the heroine. Everyone thought it must be daily fare in Milan because in the collective imagination the capital of Lombardy is the center of the Verdian repertoire and of Italian opera in general. Deep down, such expectations are right: it's good for an opera house's program to be broad and to respect the more inclusive history of music, but we also need to remember that if we're a model of anything, it is nineteenth-century Italian melodrama, and that's precisely what we're internationally recognized as—keepers of the authentic performative tradition of that time and place.

It was not an easy task: there are always lingering nostalgias, memories of untouchable performers, legends that mustn't be overshadowed, and many people prefer to hold on to those legends rather than open up to new ones. In the cultural realm, such an attitude is unquestionably illegitimate. You can't simply stop the history of performance, the natural course of new takes on old operas—operas of a "past" that is not a museum. You have to accept that the world of Callas, Tebaldi, Bastianini, and Corelli is gone and that we cannot shirk the responsibility of training new singers and giving them a go with these venerable operas.

So although my reflections suggested as much, I still knew that any name we put in the principal roles would inspire comparison with the untouchables. We had to find a new way, and I began looking for performers who could create—as it was later dubbed—a "young *Traviata*." After many auditions I chose the soprano Tiziana Fabbricini. On the one hand, she had the necessary agility, and on the other, she had a strong temperament that could give Violetta a *dramatic* virtuoso treatment, not just an empty role packed with sixteenth notes (I realize that, in the eyes of nostalgics, my words are verging on those reserved for Callas!). She had all the necessary vocal skills: virtuosity in the first act, temperament in the second, and sublimation in the third. You might like her voice or not—and, indeed, it found both admirers and detractors—but I was convinced that, on the whole and despite her youth, she could bring to light Violetta's expressive characteristics, that hint of death present as early as the first act, where the toast isn't entirely celebratory but contains (although it's usually articulated lightly) the tragic forewarning of a woman who is aware of the heavy drama within, yet tries to ignore the love that will soon overwhelm her.

The tenor, Roberto Alagna, also had an exquisite voice, full of character. Even the baritone, Paolo Coni, was very young. So, ultimately, it really was a young *Traviata*. The orchestra's expectations were filled with emotion. When I began rehearsing the overture, it couldn't have gone unnoticed that after more than a quarter century those notes were once again ringing through Piermarini's hall.[6] *Those* sounds, in *that* theater, take on a new feel, they seem more "right" there than elsewhere, and the hall reabsorbs them as if they naturally belonged to it. Meanwhile, outside those walls the voices of those who would have preferred we leave the masterpiece intact began to mount (Karajan's last performance of it was controversial even back then). I was rather astonished: I didn't understand what crime I had committed. The passion of the "nostalgics"—like all authentic passions—seemed both worthy of respect and yet culturally dangerous. Liliana Cavani was director, Dante Ferretti did the sets, Gabriella Pescucci did the costumes (the latter two are Oscar winners), and we worked a lot at the rehearsals. The setting was poetic and fit the aims of our undertaking. It may not have been the most modern *Traviata* in the world, but that wasn't what we needed right then—we just needed *La Traviata*!

My convictions were strong enough that, for once, I relaxed my notorious obduracy. On the album with Renata Scotto in the role of Violetta, at the end of the first act I had avoided the *puntatura*[7] (Toscanini had a B-flat in his recording, while the light lyric soprano tradition famously has an E-flat). During rehearsals I behaved according to my instincts and habits, but then I began to think that ending the act exactly as Verdi had written it—in a production of *La Traviata* that aimed to shatter the "wall of fear" surrounding it, and therefore demanded that my work be triumphant if I didn't want the opera to end up shelved for another twenty-six years—would have been overzealous. I asked Fabbricini to sing the E-flat, just to try it; it was full-bodied and beautiful, not the "pinpoint" sound of a sopranino. At the end of rehearsals, before going onstage, I asked her to sing it. Should I be ashamed because that contradicts my credo? Perhaps, but I needed something ravishing, and so I made a virtue of a necessity, asking Verdi's pardon. Onstage, the first act proceeded amid a singular, icy silence; I felt it literally behind my back, like the feeling I mentioned in regard to my first *Nabucco* at La Scala (that's where all the electric current comes through). It was the silence of those moved by the opera, but there was also the silence of those—I don't know how many—who were on the fence, who wanted to see how we measured up. It was exhausting for me to push onward, with two kids onstage, while the arias and cabalettas floated through the air with no response. It was like being in a soccer stadium with the players making all sorts of great moves but hearing only dead silence from the crowd. The soprano had begun the final phrases, and the orchestra, the chorus, and the dancers all wanted it to succeed, they emanated positive reinforcement as if to say, "We have to make it!" pitting the aria against the doubts of the melomaniacs. I stood there praying to Saint Ambrosius and Saint Januarius and finally Tiziana fired off an unsurpassable E-flat that, as they say, brought down the house. I'd have preferred the success to have come even without that note. The audience should also consider the less flashy achievements, the phrasing when it respects the internal physical strength of the passage and its correct "punc-tuation," the agogic accenting when it's done properly. But I was happy just the same.

The following day even the press noted something along the lines of "a dear friend has returned home." Fortunately, over the following years they echoed that sentiment on several occa-sions, and it always went well when we tapped into the "chink in the armor"[8] that we'd opened with that performance.

*

When I moved on to *Il Trovatore* in 2000, I encountered the problem of a performative praxis that often becomes outright distortion. Take, for example, the finale of act two, one of the most extraordinary moments a modern director can hope for. At a certain point, *coup de théâtre*, Manrico appears. Verdi zooms in on the soprano Leonora, who is astonished to see her beloved and poses a purely rhetorical question, "Sei tu dal ciel disceso o in ciel son io con te?" (Are you come down from heaven, or am I in heaven with you?). She looks incredulously at the man she thought was dead. Although the visual focus has shifted to Leonora, the battle—Verdi was a genius!—rages on: the warriors don't stop, the action continues. Now, as tradition would have it, at the end the tenor joins the soprano, "adjusting"— ridiculously—the libretto and singing along with her: "Son io dal ciel..." (It is I, come from heaven...). This is a terrible mistake, committed solely because, as the act draws to a close, the tenor (that is, the singer himself, an abstract, song-loving non-character—in a word: utterly anti-dramatic!) wants to sing something too, especially considering that there's a nice B-flat and he doesn't want to let it get away. But an addition like that is tantamount to giving Verdi and his extraordinary idea a slap in the face. At that instant the tenor has *nothing* to say; in the end it's the soprano who, for the last time, repeats her question to herself and the others. That kind of modification, for which so-called tradition is alone responsible, is a much graver violation than one *puntatura* more or less; here, the modernity of the situation is compromised and ultimately killed.

Such cases aren't infrequent. The famous "Mal reggendo all'aspro assalto" (At my mercy lay the foe), for example, is pianissimo in the score because Manrico is describing nothing more than an omen, a "moto arcano" or strange stirring, a voice that "vien dal cielo" (comes from heaven). But usually the opposite happens, the accompaniment rears up and roars, the tenor (again, the Tenor!) strikes a hero's pose taken straight out of "melodrama" in the less accurate and more trivial sense of the term, and delivers the lines as if they were "Hey Ma! Listen—know what I dreamt? I dreamt I really messed with that guy! Left him for dead! I was killin' him!"[9]—all said, of course, with the predictable over-gesticulation. The pianissimo has to be constant; the voice that "comes from heaven" has to assume the orchestra's dynamic *p*, which becomes *pp* with "che mi dice: Non ferir" (saying: Do not strike). It's the same as at the beginning of the second act of *La Traviata*: all the tenors sing "De' mmiei bbbollenti spirrriti, il ggiovvanil'arrdore" (Mmy pppassionate spirrrit, the fffire of yyouth) with such energy that you'd think they had a veritable Vesuvius in their lungs, spewing out fire and brimstone. He's simply saying: "Il giovanile ardore ella *temprò*" (The fire of youth she tempered). The words "passionate" and "fire" aren't the only ones that matter; the use of the term "tempered" should be a cue here!

Now, I'm not saying anyone has to sing without singing, but the singer has the obligation, through his tone, of making the listener understand that Violetta tamed and tempered his heart. I know full well that the tenor has to be the tenor and we can't afford to emasculate Alfredo, to deprive him of the boldness that almost always characterizes him, but there he's saying something else, something quite different from when someone sings without thinking about what he's saying. That sounds like a play on words, but it aptly describes the contradictory situation singers can get caught up in when they lose their judgment.

Unfortunately Verdi's works as they are staged, because of the importance of the voice—an importance I don't question in the least—are full of such misunderstandings. We must never forget what a great director and man of the theater he was: with his scores, he recommends conductors do as he's written. If at a given point in the manuscript score for *Il Trovatore* he's written *pppppppppppp* (*piano* twelve times over) it's certainly an exaggeration driven by the fear that the conductor wouldn't even grant it a *pp*; and maybe he jotted down the extra ten *p*s during rehearsals, when he got tired of begging! We have to heed his fundamental directions, just as we have to when conducting Beethoven, where unfortunately and all too often *f* and *ff* are performed in the same exact way, thereby eliminating the sudden violent bursts that mark his music's characteristic surprise.

Consider *Macbeth*, the opera where Verdi achieves an enigmatic *mute sound*! The maestro has to maintain the sound's terrible "Verdian" vibration, but also has to create something new; over the course of my artistic life, I have tried. I may have made mistakes, and that would pain me. If one day in the great beyond Wagner or Beethoven or Spontini were to tell me, "You were wrong, Riccardo!" I'd be able to take it, but if Verdi were to tell me that—Verdi, to whom I gave my devoted love, and for whom I stood ready to retreat into an ideal orchestra pit and disappear—it would be terrible. I've always tried to impress—or, rather, make Verdi impress—the audience, not just viscerally, but *totally*.

The same problem comes up in *Il Trovatore* in the funeral pyre scene, at the end of which I avoided the full-chested C that Verdi *didn't* write. I tried this for the first time in Florence, with the extraordinary audience that had always tried to follow me or at least understand my intent. I had my reasons: Manrico's part is completely central to the opera (aside from a B-flat and a few duets with the soprano where, so to speak, the high note ends up in parentheses, beginning with the trio in the first act). And that character is not a warrior but a poet, even if he sometimes ends up in battle. But Italians never really think about it and sometimes, intimidated and weighed down by "tradition," we make mistakes without meaning to. If anyone asks what we're going to see this evening, we stand tall and proudly reply, "*Il Trrrovatore!*" as if we were enthusiastically saying, "Ettore Fieramosca!"[10] when we should simply say, "*Il Trovatore.*" Conversely, the following evening we might wanly mumble, "*La Tra . . . ia . . . ta,*" when instead we should show a bit more realism and reply firmly. Indeed, the opera becomes incomprehensible if you forget that Violetta is, albeit at a very high level, nothing more than a prostitute. Pronouncing *La Traviata* sweetly and *Il Trovatore* with an aggressive frown means distorting them beginning with the very title.

The famous C also calls for a series of "adjustments." At the end of the cabaletta in act three ("Di quella pira l'orrendo foco") Manrico sings the dominant G at the same time the chorus sings "All'armi." During that G—marked *tenor tenet* (the tenor holds)—fifteen beats from the end, the orchestra and chorus alternate the dominant and tonic harmonies (which that note indifferently belongs to: first *G*-B-D, second C-E-*G*). If, however, you want to perform the C, you can get away with it through the tonic *C*-E-G, but then you butt up against the dominant G-B-D, which doesn't call for it. It's true that in some cases the tenor—who has already corrected a G as a C with the words "col sangue vostro" (with your blood)—politely waits for the tonic harmony the chorus ends with, but some tenors, even a few famous ones, begin to show off the high note too early, on the chorus's dominant harmony. So, according to tradition, the tenor should sing that note *after* the chorus has finished, which is still overturning what Verdi wrote. Also—and this is something I really cannot stand—it's often a way for the tenor to catch and save his breath for the final C, so to that end he's *silent* through the entire part Verdi wrote to place him in "dialogue" with the chorus.

Then they draw the curtains, the tenor grabs onto the C and the curtain, and sometimes, if he still has the energy, even opens the curtain again and then closes it again, all while the orchestra is playing as long as the trumpets and everyone else still has some breath left! In order to do this, as I said, you have to change what's written in the score, and in the meantime—while the flames have reached Azucena's knees!—the chorus just stands there. Some will say: back then they made it an *acuto*, a high note. However, I know, and so did Verdi himself, that back then he had no power to stop it. Don't you think that, if he'd wanted to change that note from a G to a C, he'd have done it in 1857 when he revised the score for Paris and, in the process, made a lot of modifications, both major and minor? I'm not at all questioning whether it's pleasing or exciting, I'm just pointing out that in order to enjoy that here you have to drastically alter the musical course of the work. And it gets worse. Many tenors want to do the C, but some of them, in order to avoid any disagreement and keep calm, force the maestro to bring everything down a half tone, or even a whole tone. The audience goes home having heard its beloved "C" and doesn't know it was only a B-flat, and in this way the overall harmonic plan of a whole series of scenes is ruined. I remember that, the day after the first *Il Trovatore* at La Scala, during a radio transmission they played many different recordings of the pyre scene, and the radio host kept on breezily talking about the C when it was evident that the anthology they were playing contained various Bs and B-flats! It happens: oftentimes we professionals are forced to listen to the "experts" discoursing, and I assure you it requires great patience.

*

In *Rigoletto* a lot of the baritone's soaring parts are arbitrary decisions absent in the original manuscript. But I have to say, while with *Il Trovatore* there were a few small protests, that didn't happen in 1994 with *Rigoletto*, which had also long suffered from the performers' added pomp, even though it is among Verdi's finest works and, as he wrote in a famous letter, almost "without arias." You could perform it from start to finish without any interruption—that is, without the interruptions caused by the audience's applause after every such "number."

Let's take the example of "La donna è mobile" and, again, its conclusion. The tenor usually shows off the high note like a Heldentenor unsheathing his sword. Now, it's true that a little further along Verdi wrote a B-natural, but only for when the duke falls asleep lightly singing offstage (which by contrast should be performed pianissimo and diminuendo because it signals someone sliding into sleep). In this case things are even clearer than in the pyre scene, and the proof I gave when I explained it at La Scala, comparing it to the French version, seems incontrovertible. Since Verdi calls for a B-natural two pages later at that same point in the melody, had he really wanted it earlier as well, he would have written it in. And another thing to consider: with the words "viver dee o morire" (is he to live or die?) a bassoon plays on and returns to the song's main theme playing *ppp*, drawing out a long B-natural, so the composer's intent was that, before this coda, the music wasn't to be interrupted by applause—which would only be triggered by a high note, since, if I may borrow a phrase from the world of advertising, certain opera audiences obey the rule *No acuto, no applausi!* (No high note, no hand!). Furthermore, the B, the melody's conclusion, is an important note from a harmonic point of view as well, inasmuch as it is the dominant of the next tonality, the E major in which the famous quartet "Un dì, se ben rammentomi" (One morn, if I remember well) is performed. If the tenor's high note hinders the orchestra's playing and the bassoon's magical suspension, it all falls apart. Doesn't that strike you as a crime? I'd prefer to wait a bit, hear the note offstage after a few minutes, and let things run just as a musician of Verdi's greatness envisioned them.

A little later Rigoletto sings "un sacco il suo lenzuolo. All'onda! All'onda!" (a sack his winding sheet. To the river! To the river!). As it's traditionally played, the second time calls for a *puntatura* that, out of sheer anticipation, leads him to suddenly forget that he's a hunchback. That's odd behavior; at that moment he should be thinking only of getting rid of the duke's body, without making all of Mantua hear his high note, if you will. Mind you, I don't want to stifle the audience's passion for beautiful notes, but by following that instinct we use Verdi as a means to other ends.

One last case is "Mi coglierà sventura? Ah no: è follia" (Will some disaster befall me? Ah no, this is folly!). The baritone generally unfurls a G-natural on the word "follia," preferably after he's raised his hand like some ancient Roman orator. He'd do well to obey the maxim of the great baritone Mattia Battistini: "Never promise with the hand what you cannot deliver with the voice," and above all he'd do well to avoid that high note. Where the first line says "tal pensiero perché conturba ognor la mente mia?" (why should this thought still prey so on my mind?), Verdi wrote *ppp* precisely because he's talking about a thought, and the following *interior* volley of lines that all take place within his tormented conscience should be sung the same way: "Mi coglierà sventura? Ah no: è follia." Rigoletto meditates, albeit in a hurry, all wrapped up in himself, and, from a theatrical point of view, when such anxious doubt ends up in a shout, it sounds ridiculous.

There's another flaw: that G-natural means that the explosion of the C major in the orchestra that introduces the duet between Gilda and Rigoletto is literally drowned out by the audience's roar (because of the equation mentioned above: one high note = a thousand people clapping). It's a curtain of sorts that opens onto the soprano's unexpected entrance, the arrival of the daughter, of joy, of light, and another incredibly impressive *coup de théâtre*. The "shoddy effect" (of the high note, likely followed by applause) cancels out the sublime effect (of Gilda) and turns the orchestral introduction, which is more or less inaudible, into a frivolous, vague grumbling.

In all truth, Rigoletto really is a grandiose figure, something other than the A-flat with which baritones end the revenge scene. There are other minor details that tradition has corrupted, and some have even made it into the libretto. The Duke of Mantua, for example, a ruthless libertine with a chronic case of infidelity like some provincial Don Juan, comes in toward the end and—according to the version performed in theaters over several decades—orders Sparafucile to procure "Una stanza e del vino" (A room and some wine), upon which Rigoletto and Gilda comment, "Son questi i suoi costumi!" (Such are the fellow's habits!) and Sparafucile exclaims, "Oh, il bel zerbino!" (Oh, what a dandy!).[11] If that's really what he requested, I have to ask: what would be so wrong with that? That's like walking into a hotel at ten in the evening and asking, "Excuse me, could you give me a room, please? And could you have a bottle of wine sent up as well?" only to hear the receptionist mumble, "What unsavory folk are out and about at this hour of the night." There's more to it: the Duke of Mantua in the original libretto actually asked for "Due cose e tosto: tua sorella e del vino" (Two things, and quick: your sister, and some wine), a request the censors understandably found somewhat lacking in decency, so they "corrected" Piave's text. Remember, Verdi wasn't the satisfied guarantor of such performative praxis, but rather its victim.

One evening, in the archive collections at La Scala, I happened to see a poster for an evening performance held not long after the opera's 1853 debut, in which the musicians performed the first act of *Il Trovatore*, followed by a fantasia of dance and fanfare, then the second act, a few new dances, no third act (the one with the pyre scene!), and finally the fourth act. Now, could anyone possibly think for even a minute that Verdi was content to see such arbitrary use made of his opera? Certainly not, so while also steering clear of fundamentalist preconceptions (for example, in some of his early operas there is a lot of variation in the use of the direction *da capo* in the arias), we must continue our quest to understand him and his work.

I'm sure that by being in favor of playing scores as written, my approach—again, by no means revolutionary just for
the sake of it, but rather straightforwardly rigorous—was the
right one. But it didn't fail to surprise audiences and spark a few
controversies in Vienna in 1983, because that was the first time
Rigoletto, which is equally popular there, was performed in a
way that respected the original, and it seemed a bit "dry" compared to the usual. At first Edita Gruberová seemed upset about
what I wouldn't let her do in the aria "Caro nome," but once
again D'Amico was on my side and had no doubts, expressing
his judgment with these peremptory words: "I have been told
she was irritated; that would be an injustice to her intellect. That
middle trill lasting two beats, which Verdi intentionally set in
that register, was perhaps the sweetest torment, the pinnacle of
the entire evening."[12] And audiences abroad ended up understanding and coming on board with me just as those in Italy had.
In Munich, Enriquez's direction of *Aida* and De Simone's direction of *Macbeth* were both a success. After the latter I even held
on to Manzù's "Neapolitan" sets.

*

When I conducted *Otello* in 2001, I lowered the diapason in order
to attain something like what Verdi requested in an 1884 letter to
Celestino Terzi, president of the Military Music Commission.
A diapason of 432,[13] the conductor wrote, "does not in the least
detract from the sonority and brio of the execution, but rather
gives it something nobler, fuller, and more majestic than can be
had from the screeches of an overly high-pitched tuning fork."[14]
Additionally, in order to reach 436 vibrations we used specially
made wind instruments. A bit earlier I wrote that the possibilities

open to us today generally weren't available to Verdi, but the years in which *Otello* was composed (it was completed in 1887, just three years after his letter to Terzi) are an exception, as he enjoyed a fame that, for practically the first time in his life, allowed him to control to some extent the way his melodramas were performed.

Such differences in pitch are minimal, and we cannot expect the audience to notice, yet they change the tone and coloration of the entire orchestra; they create a darker sound, a less brilliant gloss, and a dense tone that was certainly what the composer had in mind. (Nowadays they raise the diapason to avoid that; for a long time even the Wiener Philharmoniker had a rather high diapason, and only recently did they begin to reverse that trend.) Back then, outside the theater everyone in the city had become an expert on diapason, and they ventured opinions with a frankness I'd never have if I were to suddenly start talking about ophthalmology. They said it was done to ease the singers' task and make them more comfortable, but that's wrong, because such a minute distinction wouldn't be enough to worry a tenor or soprano.

I had real difficulty finding the right Otello. I suddenly thought of Plácido Domingo, whom I had met while conducting *Aida* in Vienna in 1973 and with whom I'd worked for many years, and luckily he accepted. Graham Vick was the director, and his approach, using a large cylinder at center stage, showed all the signs of a true artist as soon as the curtains parted. It's his trademark to fill the set in a way that visually clarifies the story for the audience, which all too often (understandably, given the linguistic and other barriers) doesn't know exactly what's going on. Vick places the point of reference right in front of you, and it strikes me as a very effective way to seduce the viewers. There's no need for them to understand everything immediately—they'll get it as the various acts and events unfold. But this gives them a compass of sorts or, to phrase it better, given the massive size of the sets, a lighthouse well within their grasp. Four years earlier, in 1997, he had already done *Macbeth* with me at La Scala, and that time there was a bright cube at the center of the stage, establishing it as a peculiarly mental environment, a psychological landscape. It reminded me of what Proust said when he wrote that all great artists do the same thing over and over again; even in Stendhal's various novels there is always a key donjon—a highly visible tower, as it were, that serves as a point of reference for the reader. Once I saw a video recording of Rossini's *Ermione*, also directed by Vick, and again there a large iron tower dominated the stage. In the end Domingo was a great success, even though he fell ill during the second act of the second performance and had to quit.

*

In 2004 *Otello* was followed, as is only fitting, by *Falstaff*. When I was still a young conductor in Florence, I happened to discuss the work with Gui. "Be careful," he said. "When you conduct it, you must never forget that it is a chamber opera." He advised that I maintain a bit of lightness throughout, beginning with the first measures, when there's a full-orchestra fortissimo that almost inevitably risks becoming too heavy. When I conducted it at La Scala (with Strehler directing) and again in Busseto (directed by Cappuccio, but with the sets designed for Toscanini's performance of the work there in 1913 and 1921), I held myself to that principle. I'm particularly fond of the *Falstaff* we performed in the small town of Busseto.[15] Although the number of winds stayed the same, I had reduced the strings to five first violins, five second violins, four violas, three cellos, and two double basses, to create the type of ensemble that makes the opera work markedly better: through that trimming you obtain an almost twentieth-century sound, something that sounds a bit like Stravinsky but well before his time.

In my search for the lead singer I discovered the impressive Ambrogio Maestri, who has a wonderfully frank, quintessentially Italian baritone voice, a bit like Giangiacomo Guelfi's. He played the role with great intellect, with lightness despite its sheer tonnage, and to this day he's the absolute best any conductor can hope for to play Falstaff. I was impressed by his very first audition, when he sang "Eri tu" from *Un ballo in maschera*. During intermission of the debut performance I ran to ask him how he felt. He turned to me and, with his trademark Pavia attitude and accent, said with a touch of irony: "Maestro, if you go on like this, we run the risk of putting on a nice little show."[16]

*

When I did *Don Carlos*, the newspapers were all over it, especially because of Pavarotti's presence. The great tenor was often associated with the brightness of his extraordinary high notes, but there was another Pavarotti who was less garish and more delicate, with noteworthy phrasing abilities. It's unfair to make the famous "Vincerò" his theme song, as happened both for the 1990 World Cup and for his funeral in September 2007. I might have chosen something different, or I would at least have liked to hear his voice sing "Ma lassù ci vedremo" (But we will see one another up there). Anyone who was at La Scala in 2005 will remember the richness of his voice—even in the pianissimos it had an undeniable elegance and expressivity—and can't but grant him recognition for his many qualities that went unacknowledged, or were heavily overshadowed by the boldness and sheer heat of his performances.

He accepted the role of Don Carlos with a bit of reluctance, but in the end I convinced him and he studied the opera for me. He gave the rehearsals, both alone and with the orchestra, real dedication, discipline, and desire to do well. He gave it his all and, whenever his memory lapsed, he opened the score that had become a permanent fixture under his arm. That innocent behavior of his—he thought he was surrounded only by benevolent souls!—triggered a rumor outside that he didn't know the opera and was stumbling more and more as the rehearsals progressed. That way those who didn't love him—we all have friends and enemies, fans and detractors—simply deepened their prejudices. It really saddens me today to remember how someone with the courage to check the score in front of everyone could be so maligned. (Besides, didn't Richter read in his old age, too? And wasn't he a first-rate pianist?) On opening night, when he came to an acute that was supposed to be a B-natural, he missed the note by a hair. Part of the audience let out a loud protest, and once the theater heated up, the other singers began to pay for the minor incident as well. I considered it, and still do, a somewhat unfair reaction to an artist who had given a lot to the world of opera, an artist who had been *the* Tenor. For better or worse, only history can pass judgment on his interpretations. But anyone who listens to the album will hear proof of

Pavarotti's strengths. Obviously, nothing in this world is perfect, but from an artistic point of view, given his dedication and aim to capture the character, that performance, it must still be said, is absolutely praiseworthy.

Luciano was also a large-hearted man. Once there was a community effort to aid the recovery of drug addicts in the province of Forlì, and the priest who spearheaded it asked Cristina to help in getting past a few obstacles. She called Luciano, and figured I could be an accompanying pianist. He came without asking for a dime, and in the Forlì sports arena we did a concert that was also professionally recorded. (Those recordings were never commercially released, as we didn't want to improperly capitalize on the event.) The first piece was Gluck's aria "Che farò senza Euridice," and I was thrilled as I reflected that it was quite far from Luciano's style and repertoire. Then we did Tosti and Cilea, and Puccini, where he was amazing. So, on a human level, Pavarotti was capable of great generosity.

The unfair reception of that *Don Carlos* also upset me on behalf of the entire production; from Zeffirelli's direction to the cast as a whole, it was undoubtedly an "important" staging. So my relationship to this world-famous tenor was excellent, and the friction that had arisen nearly twenty years earlier as we prepared to perform *I puritani* at La Scala—a production I ended up canceling during the penultimate rehearsal—was entirely a thing of the past.

*

I'd also like to talk about the night of June 2, 1995, when I "conducted" the entire "orchestra" of *La Traviata* from the piano bench because of a strike. Newspapers around the globe wrote about it, even the local paper in San Antonio, Texas. It went like this: It was a Friday, the theater was packed, and a lot of foreigners were in the crowd. At the time tense union negotiations filled the air, and no solutions had been reached. An orchestra assembly had met that morning, at which I tried to dissuade them out of respect for the audience, and that afternoon they met with mayor Gabriele Albertini. They didn't come to an agreement, and just half an hour before the concert was scheduled to start, with the audience already taking its seats, La Scala's general manager, Carlo Fontana, told me that because of the strike the performance wasn't to take place. No one had notified me in time. Everything else was ready; the only thing missing was the orchestra. We conductors are left "mute" without an orchestra, so you can only imagine how I, Maestro Muti, felt—doubly mute, both by surname and by circumstance! Fontana walked out onstage and stood before the orchestra pit—deserted as it was, it looked frightfully empty—and he was interrupted after just a few words. Had it been a play, the script would have read: "Unfortunately I must break the bad news that . . . [*shouts from the furious audience*]."

I was still in my dressing room all decked out in my conducting clothes, while the audience in the concert hall stood their ground with no signs of budging, as if ready to set the theater ablaze—and I can't say they were wrong. I was getting advice from all sides, from the general manager to the artistic director and many others; a few suggested I solve the problem by putting a pianist in the pit to substitute for the orchestra, with me conducting him from the podium! I didn't want to take any of their suggestions, which really were implausible. I shut myself in my dressing room, sad and pained that it was the orchestra that was on strike while the rest of the company was ready to go on stage. Looking at it through the eyes of public opinion, I felt a responsibility for something I hadn't the least guilt in. And I didn't know what to do. Every once in a while I glanced at the closed-circuit television that showed the hall; in the boxes and upper tiers it looked like an infernal madhouse, and on the orchestra floor like a valley of lost souls aimlessly roaming about. Amid all that discouragement and desperation I heard a voice from afar—it sounded like Cristina's, and she was out of town that night—telling me, "You play, Riccardo."

I suddenly jumped up, opened the door, and announced that I would play the orchestra's part on the piano. I asked that the audience not be told until I could be sure my plan would be physically possible. I ran up and asked if there were a piano backstage, and they told me that the one normally used for concerts had been moved somewhere else earlier that day—panic! Gino Salvi, the orchestra manager who oversees every aspect of the ensemble's organization, came to the rescue: there was a baby grand, he said, out by the singers' dressing rooms. I rushed to check that it had the bare necessities for such an undertaking; it wasn't ideal, but it would do. So I had it moved to center stage while the curtains were still tightly drawn. They positioned it where I wanted, but then we encountered an unexpected problem: because the stage was slanted, it began to roll toward the pit. The stagehands ran up and quickly hammered some wedges around the wheels, which finally stayed put while my heartbeat grew ever faster. I didn't know that in the meantime—against my wish that the audience not be told just yet—the ushers had been unleashed outside the theater to go and find those members of the audience who had gone to nearby restaurants on the assumption the performance would be canceled. Meanwhile, as the ushers ran to invite the audience back, the singers were already in costume, as were the dancers and the whole chorus.

But the surprises weren't over. The chorus committee came to see me; they didn't agree with my decision. "I have every intention," I told them, "of performing the opera, if the audience is amenable to the idea, even if it means performing without the chorus." The choristers, though they weren't officially part of the strike, left the theater. So now I had to face the audience, and from behind the curtain I could already hear their murmuring, which felt as urgent as "the infernal hurricane, that never resteth."[17] When I appeared, the shouting seemed to rise up in an immediate crescendo and then suddenly dissolve into a long, deafening silence. Clearly everyone was wondering what I was about to say. Pointing to the orchestra pit, which was empty save for six musicians who had decided not to strike, I addressed the audience, expressing my regret that it would be impossible to perform the opera without the orchestra. The silence grew more deafening still. A moment went by that felt like an eternity, and I ventured my idea: I would perform the opera myself, at the piano, along with the lead singers. I asked the audience's forgiveness in advance should my fingers miss a note or two (though I was in fairly good shape, as I'm used to spending hours at the keyboard when rehearsing with the singers). A unanimous shout of approval rose from the audience. The corps de ballet stayed on, which was a great advantage because they all sat on the seats and sofas that were part of the set; grouped around the piano like that, they helped the stage feel more like Violetta Valéry's sitting room.

I began, naturally, with the overture. Although the chorus's absence meant we had to skip a few parts, such as the aria "Si ridesta in ciel l'aurora," the evening progressed quite well, and the leads, energized by the peculiar situation, seemed even more transported than usual as they sang. At the end of the second act I announced the intermission, as would happen in any performance. This gave me time to return to my dressing room and go through the score's tougher sections one more time. I blessed my old teacher, Maestro Vincenzo Vitale, who all those years ago in Naples had made the piano my close acquaintance through his futuristic do-mi-re-fa exercises. Meanwhile, La Scala's press office had called RAI to notify them of the unusual concert, and the television crews showed up as swiftly as firefighters. At the end of the performance, the applause seemed it might never end.

I firmly believed in my decision, and the audience clearly understood that. But later that night, when it was all over, I wasn't happy. I felt there was something awry, and so I called a press conference the following morning. I held it in the Sala Gialla, the so-called Yellow Hall, the historic room that Toscanini used, where all the greatest singers from Callas on have performed, which was demolished a few years ago during the theater's renovation, committing a senseless crime against history and therefore culture as well. I remember saying that, although they wanted to portray me as the victorious hero, no one had won the night before and, despite the emotions the performance inspired, it had to be considered a sad day in which the theater, the orchestra, I myself, Verdi, and the audience, who had still only experienced a "diminished" opera, had all lost out. I also explained that my intervention in extremis wasn't an act against the orchestra but rather a decision dictated by my desire not to spoil the audience's festive energy, and I reminded everyone that music mustn't be gagged.

I'm convinced that—despite the many joyous years that followed, which were as productive as the years before—that evening broke some of the trust I had with the orchestra, or at least a part of it.

*

Speaking of the Sala Gialla, the great artists who performed there, and the bitterness left behind by its hasty destruction in 2002, I have to tell you about my reverent farewell to that space. When the theater closed down for renovations and we moved to the Teatro degli Arcimboldi, my office was one of the last in the old theater to remain open. All the seats were ripped out, and once the "iron curtain"[18] was torn down, the main hall had a spectral feeling, with only the central "core" remaining aglow.

One morning a woman named Valentina Cortese knocked on my door. She was a devoted regular at La Scala and had grown up in the audience (she adored the conductor Victor De Sabata). She told me how hard it was for her to see the old theater go. I walked with her a while, and she stopped at the side stair when she felt a pang in her heart. When I stepped back to look at her from afar, she went to stand under the faint lamplight and, in total silence, slowly began to almost dance. That day she wore a light white dress, and her movements seemed to me to have the cadence of a sacrifice to the theater that was nearing the end. It reminded me of the "Sacrificial Dance" from the *Rite of Spring*.[19] I can't quite describe it, but it seemed like a dream. We went back to my dressing room together and she asked if she could have something as a souvenir. In the end, on one of the proscenium platforms at stage left (her usual side), we found a small mantelpiece whose red velvet was frayed. Although it was worthless and would soon be bound for the Dumpster, we asked permission to hang on to it, and she took it home with her. A few days later—in a letter that affectionately began "Splendid rascal from the fiery South, my dearest free-and-easy friend, beguiling and irresistible maestro"[20]—she wrote to me to express her poetic thanks, telling me about her "memories of devastatingly beautiful, delirious harmonies that consumed one's soul," going on to say "sometimes the musical current that flowed from the orchestra was so rarefied that it seemed they were playing with air and light, and other times one was overcome by a spasmodic flurry of one incandescent note after the other with such an implacable rhythmic violence that the chords seemed like screams that would never end. You see, that mantelpiece now holds my entire youth, my dreams, my expectations, my desires, and my tears."

Of the modern productions, I remember with particular emotion Salvatore Sciarrino's *La morte di Borromini*, with Tino Carraro as the narrating voice, as well as many works we commissioned from contemporary composers: Giacomo Manzoni, Luca Francesconi, Fabio Vacchi, Ivan Fedele, Eliodoro Sollima. Of the classical productions, my most important project was perhaps the staging of all of Beethoven's nine symphonies in 1997–98. It had been a long time since an undertaking like that had distinguished La Scala's program, and I tried to schedule them all within a fairly narrow window so the audience could reflect upon and compare the various works.

*

With La Scala and its philharmonic I performed worldwide at the broadest range of theaters imaginable. I remember doing Verdi's *Requiem* in Paris—we were in Notre-Dame, with a massive screen above the sacristy—and concerts in East and West Berlin when they were still divided by the Wall. During our first trip to Japan, Carlos Kleiber came with me and directed *La Bohème*. We'd become good friends and remained close until his death. There's a photograph taken of us in Salzburg during one of my rehearsal breaks while preparing a Bruckner symphony with the Wiener Philharmoniker; we were seated in the music hall and, as a joke when they asked us to sign it, we switched things around and wrote our names under one another's picture.

I also recorded a lot with the Filarmonica della Scala, primarily live recordings made in the course of various performances and concerts. I prefer live recording because, especially with melodrama, I've always found it terribly hard to dredge up inspiration just as the producer says, "Stand by ... Ready!" and the little red light turns on. "It's strange ... it's strange ...": what's strange is that we have to say that just then because they're telling us to, and—as if that weren't enough—we have to say it in English! I won't go into the whole rich catalogue of symphonic recordings we did. I also considered it important that our concert seasons were recorded by Rete4 (Channel 4) and aired on television, and I was sad to hear that, after I left, that tradition came to an end.

*

During my years with La Scala I had a marvelous encounter with Elizabeth II, queen of England. We met in 2000, as I was conducting a concert with a mixed English and Italian program that purposely included Elgar's *In the South* (*Alassio*). After the applause, the strict protocol of Buckingham Palace required that I pay a respectful visit to the queen, but it was instead she who came to my dressing room; the route to get there was unbelievably long, twisted, and even dangerous for anyone over twenty. I urgently asked Lord Weinstock how I should comport myself. Instead of "Your Majesty" he suggested I say "Ma'am." To my ears that sounded something like "Mèemma mia!"[21]—the way an Apulian would say "Mamma mia!"—and I figured I'd have quite a time getting that out! I was embarrassed to say so, and then I heard the rustling sound of her retinue coming down the hall. I stood in the doorway and, remembering that there was a dangerous step right in front of my door, I started off by gesturing to the queen. While I mumbled something highly respectful, it was neither "Ma'am" nor "Majesty," but rather— in the fear she might trip—more or less the standard "*Attenzione,* look out!" The queen must have understood I lacked the proper manners, and the photos taken of us just then caught us both in irrepressible laughter. The meeting was supposed to last seven minutes, at first with Milan's Mayor Albertini, and then just the three of us: the queen, the prince consort, and me (in recognition of the period I'd spent in London, I believe). But Weinstock and his wife came in as well, and we stayed behind closed doors for twenty-three minutes. She struck me as an unaffected woman, regal yet friendly with her interlocutor. Before she left she named me Knight Commander of the British Empire. (The official appointment was sent to the ministry in Rome, where it sat for a few months, and was then forwarded to Milan, where it was handed to me unceremoniously by the receptionist.)

*

The end of my relationship with La Scala was a tempestuous affair for many reasons, none of which had anything to do with the artistic understanding I shared with the orchestra and chorus, which was always excellent. It was as turbulent as any storm that comes on quickly. I don't want to think about it, and I prefer to focus instead on the marvelous and, as many have said, particularly lively period in which my life joined with that of the theater.

CHAPTER EIGHT

The Neapolitan Spirit

As you might easily imagine, one theater I've always had a special relationship with—from an artistic point of view not unmixed with purely human curiosity—is the Teatro San Carlo in Naples. My first contact there was the theater's first postwar director, Pasquale Di Costanzo. The Americans had appointed him; he'd previously run a business selling mattresses, and he was tall, handsome, and the epitome of Mediterranean charm. He brought remarkable progress to the theater, as evidenced by the 1950 debut of *Wozzeck*, performed for the first time on an Italian stage in the original German, conducted by Karl Böhm. The theater was Di Costanzo's home—not that he reigned despotically there, but it was simply the object of his most scrupulous care and affection.

He invited me there when I won the Cantelli Competition, and I brought a program that included Bellini, Tchaikovsky, and Strauss. I chose Strauss's difficult and virtuosic *Aus Italien* (From Italy) above all for its last two movements, "Am Strande von Sorrent" and "Neapolitanisches Volksleben," which quotes "Funiculì-funiculà," the popular song composed just before Strauss arrived in Italy. In the symphonic poem it is presented with all the cement you might expect in a plainly Teutonic harmonization (even if it did unleash the orchestra to perform rapid, electrifying passages). When we met, Di Costanzo wanted to give me just five rehearsals, and I complained that the piece wasn't in the orchestra's repertoire, so doing it with so little practice would be impossible. "Maestro," he said to me with peremptory kindness, "let's think about this a bit: Bellini's symphony is a trifle, and we'll slide through it in one second; Tchaikovsky's concerto is part of our repertoire, so we'll whip it into shape with one rehearsal. After that, Strauss: one rehearsal, and you'll read *From Italy* with the orchestra. By the third rehearsal you'll have established your personality, so that's three in all. Maestro, you've got one extra rehearsal."[1] Only the dress rehearsal was left: I made haste to thank him and, out of fear he'd deny me yet another, fled from the theater.

We did those rehearsals: in the first movement, "Auf der Campagna," there's a marvelous melody with an unparalleled sense of place; in the second, "In Roms Ruinen," things grew a bit more complicated, but we pushed forward. The third is titled "Am Strande von Sorrent." "Is what's written on the parts clear?" I asked the orchestra musicians, and one replied, "Who here knows French?"[2] It was a joke I smiled, and translated: "On the Beach at Sorrento." After fifteen seconds of unsettling silence in which everyone was apparently thinking the same thing, a violist stood up and asked, "Since when has Sorrento had a beach?"[3] I was brought up short as for the first time I realized that, indeed, the whole town is perched atop a steep and craggy cliff and has no proper beach. So our fine Neapolitan musician had called out Strauss, who was summoning almost impressionistic sonorities to describe something that particular place doesn't even have.

To their eyes he must have seemed like a phony or a liar. The concert was a success, and as always the audience gave us an incredibly warm welcome—after all, they knew full well that I was born in Naples, in the neighborhood called Chiaia, on Via Cavallerizza 14, to a *napoletanissima* mother.

*

Another time I conducted *Ivan the Terrible*, and I told them that on the album I had used a recording of the actual bells at the Kremlin. So I required real bells. During the read-through, when the time came, I heard the unmistakable sound of a tubular bell, *Tun! tun! tun! tun!*

I stopped and exclaimed, "Those are supposed to be the bells of the Kremlin?"

Everyone fell into turmoil. "The maestro wants the bells!"[4]

"I'm not the one who wants them, it's written right here!"

"Well, these are them."

"No, I want real bells and I said as much before."

Then the director gestured to a stagehand and said, "Listen, there's a metal sheet way up there; go bring the metal sheet down."[5]

So that's how it ended up, with that metal sheet that they evidently kept around to make thunder when Wagner called for a *Donnermaschine*—it was all like a Totò film, even if some other bells miraculously appeared as well. For me, these are some of the fondest memories I have of the most beautiful theater in the world, where Rossini was musical director for several years.

The orchestra musicians were full of passion. I remember once we had to play a passage with long pizzicatos. The art of the pizzicato isn't as easy as you'd think. If you just go *pling*

pling pling with your finger, the result is expressionless; as I once found myself saying during a rehearsal of the theme for the variations in the *Eroica*, it sounds like you're listening to someone distractedly tossing four pebbles into a pond, *plunk, plunk, plunk, plunk*. An old musician in the last row voiced a suggestion in dialect to his younger colleagues: "Guaglio', 'a carne!"— "Don't forget the fleshy part of your fingertips, guys."

The world I experienced at the Teatro San Carlo is a marvelous one that is disappearing, and for me every memory of it is enchanting. I even felt it was a little bit "my" theater as well—I shared its style and its sense of humor (of course, there were other aspects I appreciated somewhat less). I conducted *Macbeth* there in 1984, with Mario Sequi directing and sets by Manzù, who chose a dominant white that, by antithesis, took on a funereal tone. My work with the orchestra was particularly intense, and the outcome was, technically speaking, impeccably correct.

I went back with the Philadelphia Orchestra, the Wiener Philharmoniker, the Filarmonica della Scala, and most recently the Berliner Philharmoniker. Everyone told me how amazed they were by the sheer splendor and acoustic efficiency of the hall, which filled me with a deep pride. I became even more convinced that it's the most beautiful hall in the world, and that the entire history of opera, in terms of places and traditions, is Italian. Indeed, in Italy we don't have isolated reference points like Covent Garden in London, or the Opéra de Paris and the Opéra Garnier; rather, we have an infinite number of halls, which is why Bellini and his contemporaries wrote their operas with the so-called *prima esecuzione assoluta* in mind, the "absolute first performance." In Italy it would be impossible to think of maintaining only two or three institutions: all the grand historic theaters have to be looked after with the same care—Turin, Genoa, Venice, Bologna, Florence, Palermo, Catania. . . . For us to save just one or two would be an antihistorical approach; it would be tantamount to fragmenting what might well be the future source of our pride as citizens of the country that Bruno Barilli called "the country of melodrama," and that I would call the land of lyric opera houses.

CHAPTER NINE

Encounters

URING my world travels I've met many, many people, but if I were asked to characterize what it's like to be a professional musician, the first thing that comes to mind is that it's a solitary pursuit—like a mission, a sacrifice. The musician is alone: alone in his quest for the ideal interpretation, alone before the score, and alone in bringing it from the page to the orchestra and from the orchestra to the audience. I think of the solitude in the dressing room before the concert and after, going over the performance in my mind, on a constant quest for perfection. For some time now, as soon as I have a day off I've been heading to Apulia by myself, to take in its centuries-old olive trees, its ruddy earth, and the castles built by Frederick II of Swabia. It's there that I rediscover the faces and voices of my past, and can pause to listen to the silences that become sources of musical inspiration.

I seek out the silence that has always been with me as I traveled the globe, like a friend to whom I can reveal many aspects of myself.

One day I wrote to my daughter, Chiara, who had decided to take up a career in the theater: "If things don't work out, it's a life of solitude and disappointment; if things do work out, it's a life of solitude and work."

That, however, doesn't take away from the fact that I've met some extraordinary people over the course of my career, and I'd like to mention some of them here.

I met John Paul II on several occasions, the first being one of his visits to La Scala. When I conducted Porpora's *Salve regina* in the Sistine Chapel, we didn't see one another, because he was ill and watched the concert from his apartment via closed-circuit television. He was different from the austere Pope Paul VI, and had more communication skills—a humanity that made him, while very great, a simple and cordial man. I have yet to meet Benedict XVI, as I've never conducted for him (although I do know that he's also a musician, and therefore saw some of my concerts in Munich and Salzburg), but I recently wrote a preface to his book *Lodate Dio con arte* (Praise God with art).

I contributed gladly, because many of the book's pages exude a sincere desire to combat the current state of decline in sacred music, now made up overwhelmingly of banal, superficial notes written for equally empty words. It's a real shame that the great centuries-long tradition of Italian sacred music, from Palestrina to Lorenzo Perosi, has been lost, especially in a country that lacks a musical heritage as popular, noble, and lively as, for example, spirituals are for Christians of color. It strikes me as a need that unfortunately hasn't taken root in the minds of many contemporary priests. We need to go back to the sacred music of the past, without having any qualms about reading the text in Latin.

The Latin language safeguards the mystical atmosphere that filled the churches I grew up in, and as a boy I never tried to make sense of it. It doesn't matter all that much to me that even back then the old folks reciting "Dies irae, dies illa" mangled the text according to the sounds of whatever dialect they spoke and didn't completely understand the meaning of what they were saying; certainly their behavior was literally "religious," being both reverent and fearful (in Latin *sacer et religiosus*, "sacred and ritual," which includes taboos). The sentimental and psychological content of the text was basically preserved intact. It would never occur to me to have the text of old or classical sacred music translated into Italian (or other languages, for that matter). I'm in favor of holding mass in Latin, if only out of a strictly personal nostalgia, certainly not because I'm a reactionary conservative. Any translation, however good it might be, will still have lost the mysticism I find so fascinating, and the believer's attention will turn instead to inexhaustible, complex concepts that would leave absolutely anyone bewildered (even the commonplace *Pater noster*). People in church often aren't thinking precisely about what they're saying—they pray, and that's it. If necessary, there could be bilingual texts with facing-page translations, like the contemporary practice of using subtitles in the theater. Is it really that important, at any given moment of the rite, as churchgoers are intent on gazing into the abyss of their own souls, that they know exactly what the words *Ave verum corpus natum de Maria virgine* mean? That's why I agreed to add four pages to Pope Ratzinger's text.

*

Of all the singers, I remember Renata Tebaldi with particular fondness. She often came to my rehearsals; she was so beautiful. She would sit down alone at the back of the theater, and I often went to speak with her during breaks. She told me how she'd have liked to work together, and I couldn't have agreed more. She was an extraordinary artist with a voice that will likely never be repeated. One day she gave me an old letter as a gift—it was from Verdi, and she had kept it on her piano for many years.

Although I never had the good fortune of meeting the woman many considered her rival, I nevertheless have an anecdote about her as well. In 1974, while planning the production of *Macbeth* to be performed the following year in Florence, I had Callas's voice in mind. I was so struck by the interpretations of hers I'd heard on albums with De Sabata that, even though I knew she had quit singing years before, I couldn't picture anyone else as Lady Macbeth. It was just a hope, nothing more: I knew full well that bringing someone who hadn't sung for more than eight years back to the stage to sing an entire opera was pure illusion. Maybe I hoped that—because of how Verdi had conceived of it, as a dramatic piece that wasn't so much sung as soulfully recited—she could rise up again as the great actress she truly was.

So one evening when I was in Philadelphia, the telephone rang, and I picked it up and heard a very warm, mysterious, deep, bewitching voice that said, "You don't know me, maestro, but I know you're looking for me."

It seemed like she was playing with that for a minute, and I didn't have the courage to reply with a banal "Who is it?"

"It's Maria Callas."

A few days before that I'd spoken with someone at EMI who worked with Angel Records, and I asked for his help in finding a lead, emphasizing how wonderful it would have been if Callas took the role. He was a good friend of hers and must have mentioned it, so Callas must have decided to indulge in this innocent game. "I'm pleased you thought of me," she continued, adding, with the tone of Violetta in the last act of *La Traviata*, "It's late."

I never met her, but I can still hear her profoundly feminine voice; for me that was something private that happened between us, and I hold on to that episode as a precious memory. And to think that she reached me through a simple telephone line: *Ordet*, the word—the voice.[1] Another legend that the passing years—*quae labitur hora*—unfortunately never gave me a chance to work with was Arthur Rubinstein, but I was told that after my first concert with the Orchestre National de France he was the first to rise for a standing ovation.

I'd also like to mention Cesare Siepi, whom I met late in his career. He was another of the artists who impressed me because they didn't make any compromises to please the immediate taste of their audience, and he did nothing that would go against the nobility his interpretations bestowed upon the work. I found similar qualities in Nicolai Ghiaurov, my Attila in Florence. He was one of those characters whose charisma you couldn't help but notice as soon as they set foot on stage; as I write this I can still picture the reactions of visible respect and amazement he received from the choristers. Unfortunately, in the theater, comparisons seem to be part of the profession's genetic makeup, and I remember everyone indulging the practice by debating who was better, Ghiaurov or Boris Christoff—who, in point of fact, had been in Florence long before, so some of them had never even heard him—all with a heat and hard-headedness reminiscent of the debate that once upon a time flared up around Fausto Coppi and Gino Bartali.[2]

I have particularly pleasant memories of Christa Ludwig and a special gesture she made. Viennese audiences viewed her as a veritable queen, and just after we finished performing Mahler's *Rückert-Lieder* they brought her a bouquet of red roses. She first went out alone to briefly take a bow and then, as we went back out to take a bow together, I noticed that a red rose had been placed, evidently by her, atop my score.

Giuseppe Di Stefano, the generous singer who inspired an insuppressible enthusiasm in his audiences—his fans included Carmelo Bene, who referred to him as Pippo in his writings and even devoted a chapter of his book to him[3]—never sang in one of my performances. Yet he worked with me in absentia, and it's a story worth telling here. We were in London, and I was recording *La Traviata* for the first time, with Renata Scotto and Alfredo Kraus singing the lead parts. I don't like to work with playbacks, which give the technicians a prerecorded "base" of the orchestral part to which they then add the singers' parts, because I strongly believe in the *hic et nunc*, the here and now, of each and every execution. But I didn't like any of the seven people EMI sent to sing the line "La cena è pronta" (Supper is served) in the second act. We were in the middle of the opera's dramatic whirlwind, with the orchestra still playing the music from the card-playing scene, and although it's just four words, they have to mirror the tone of that diabolical gyre. They then asked me, since I didn't like anyone else, if I'd sing the part myself, anonymously. But that's not my job, and I also knew that if I did, they'd be out telling the whole world the next day. So, for just those two measures, I agreed to use a playback, and before I left town I asked John Mordler, a producer at EMI and a dear friend, to find the right voice for the part. A few months later he called me and said the problem had happily been solved. Giuseppe Di Stefano had come to London almost by chance, he sang that line, and in my honor asked for only a bottle of champagne as compensation! Therefore, any of you who have those albums will realize what an accomplishment that minute vocal contribution to the scene in Flora's house really was.

I faced a similar problem with the finale of *Cavalleria rusticana*, since we were recording in London—across the Alps and more than a thousand miles from Sicily!—for the line "Hanno ammazzato compare Turiddu" (They have killed Turiddu), which probably only a southern Italian woman can sing properly. I made a few unsuccessful tries, until the day that Mordler and I walked into the recording studio in Scarlatti Hall in Naples with the prerecorded track. We had invited a popular Neapolitan actress, Isa Danieli, and when we came to that bar, she let out such a cry that the sound engineers on the other side of the glass—all English—jumped as if they'd been hit by an avalanche. Again here, as with *La Traviata*, it wasn't pedantry on my part; it was a question of capturing the part at the end of Mascagni's opera with a precision capable of sending a shiver down the audience's spine.

I also had Nicolai Gedda perform in *I puritani* and in *Guillaume Tell*. Unfortunately he did only did two performances of *Tell*. In Bellini's opera the *sortita* "A te o cara" became an incredibly noble *Lied* and led me to notice, for the first time, a new meaning in those lines: love would bring about a truce between the two factions. He imbued the melody with such serenity that it seemed to fill the entire theater; he landed the high note on "se rammento" with great consistency—that is, consistent with

Bellini, who marked a ritardando (*stentando*) immediately after but not during the highest note, and thus, by eliminating any further delay before the C-sharp, avoided any temptation on the tenor's part to show off.

Of all the soloists I've met, Sviatoslav Richter became a particular friend. He loved many lesser-known orchestral works, and he had a passion—both public and private—for the surprising. He was careful to avoid any opinion that had the air of an *idée reçue*. For example, if someone—predictably—praised Masaccio or Raphael, he'd mention Sassetta. When talking about various cities, if people named Florence, Siena, Rome, or Venice, he was delighted to name—with a touch of snobbery—towns that no one there had ever heard of; once he replied, "Norcia!" It was the same with music: he loved a "surprise" and always sought out an unforeseeable cadenceor unexpected modulation and focused on it. He applied this philosophy to everyday life, too. Once he decided to bring flowers to my wife Cristina, and just before he arrived he removed the wrapping and hid them behind his back so as to present them to her at the last moment with an unexpected and incredibly elegant gesture.

I was deeply moved by something Richter once did when we were at the Genoa train station shortly after a concert. We had performed Ravel's *Concerto for the Left Hand*. He'd had a moment of amnesia, and I managed to keep the orchestra under control as he caught himself before the slip became noticeable to the audience. He was really upset, and in order to regain his composure he asked to repeat the entire concerto as an encore (it doesn't even run to twenty minutes, and had been received enthusiastically by the audience). During the endless applause a few orchestra members approached him and me backstage to say they weren't thrilled by the idea of repeating the whole piece, but I threatened to reopen their complaint *coram populo*, in the presence of the public; the protest subsided, we went back in, and it all went swimmingly. The next day as we were waiting for our train to Florence, Richter came over to me, asked for the score, flipped through the pages, stopped at the exact passage he'd forgotten, and carefully signed his name next to it. "I wanted to sign my name here," he said, "because I want you to remember, every time, that this is where *I messed up.*" It was an exemplary lesson in humility from a truly great artist.

*

I would also like to mention Robert Casadesus, with whom, very early in my career, I did Saint-Saëns's Fourth Piano Concerto at the RAI auditorium in Milan. Back then there were still a few of the old grand ensembles. I knew the Orchestra Scarlatti quite well from my time in Naples, and as a student I had gone to their rehearsals to hear legends like Pierre Monteux, Sergiu Celibidache, and Charles Munch; the Orchestra di Roma, which I had also worked with early on and which had truly first-rate musicians like Severino Gazzelloni, Domenico Ceccarossi, Giuseppe Selmi, and Angelo Stefanato. None of us could ever have imagined that such wonderful ensembles would one day vanish from Italian soil as a consequence of a sinister and wicked act![4] And senseless, too, because it happened just as the number of conservatories was increasing, training even more graduates who are then cast adrift with no land in sight.

I learned a lot when I was seated next to Casadesus: I opened the part, and on the inside cover out of the corner of my eye I saw a list of names and dates beginning in the early thirties. I peeked at where he'd recorded his performances in a beautiful and somewhat antiquated hand, and wound up—unluckily!— reading the first name: Arturo Toscanini. Once my reverential fear passed, working with him was an amazing experience. His kindness and humanity were on par with his greatness as a musician. He was one of the most high-caliber soloists I had the good fortune of working with at the very beginning of my career.

Alongside Emil Gilels I performed Beethoven's *Emperor* Concerto in Berlin with the Berliner Philharmoniker. He played the attack in the second movement at an unusually slow tempo, as if each note struggled to follow the one before it, and the orchestra musicians looked on perplexed. I waited, and when we finished I asked him about the Adagio un poco mosso and why he "thought of it" being so slow. "It's fine that way," he said, looking out into an infinite void with otherworldly eyes. "The notes should be stars shining one after the other in the firmament." He died a few months later, and when I heard the news I was ashamed that I hadn't immediately understood the suffering of a man who was already viewing music from another realm. He had completed his voyage and knew, as he spoke, that he'd reached the end; he was no longer the volcanic musician I had met on other occasions.

Paul Tortelier, however, was always volcanic, even if he was just saying "good morning." One day as we rehearsed the cello concerto by Dvořák at the Royal Festival Hall, his irrepressible enthusiasm propelled his bow across the stage, and he exploded in a supremely solicitous "Pardon!" He played as if he were improvising, and yet never lacked an absolute formal control.

I remember a similar experience with Rudolf Serkin in Philadelphia: in the first half of the *Emperor* Concerto he gave the piano a kick each time he touched the pedals. Claudio Arrau, by contrast, sticks in my mind for being as imperturbable as an icon; he had a stone-faced expression, and only his eyes showed any emotion. He was as far as you can get from today's pianists, with their tendency to flail about at the keyboard, and was castigated more harshly than anyone else even as he bestowed on the audience the sheer enchantment of his inimitable touch. His rendition of the attack in Beethoven's Fourth Piano Concerto moved me so deeply that it left me utterly perplexed: how was I then supposed to enter with the orchestra and take up the same theme? (And to think that, right before going onstage, he said to me, "Looking forward.")

After working with a first-rate soloist, isolated places in the score often come back to mind. For example, at a concert we performed in Philadelphia, Yehudi Menuhin's attack in the second movement of the Beethoven violin concerto captured precisely the "organic" aspect of the phrase as I'd learned it from Vitale and the Neapolitans; his phrasing of that Larghetto is something I'll never forget.

*

I can't end this roundup of memories without mentioning the orchestra that has given me some of my most important collaborative experiences—the Berliner Philharmoniker. I debuted with them in 1971 in a concert with Maurizio Pollini as soloist, and we played Bartók's Second Concerto, between the overture to *Guillaume Tell* and Prokofiev's Third Symphony.

From then on they invited me back each year, for increasingly long periods and for numerous, highly varied programs. I also recorded some of my favorite albums with them, beginning with Bruckner's Fourth and Sixth Symphonies, Handel's *Water Music*, Haydn's *Seven Last Words of Christ*, and many other masterpieces.

But the most beautiful of all my visits to the Philharmonie was our performance on June 23, 1980, of Carl Orff's *Carmina Burana*—a great score with stunning instrumentation. The composer was in the audience that night, and was so struck by the execution that he called it a "second premiere" of sorts (on a photo that he inscribed to me, his actual words were "mit besonderem Dank für seine gleichsam zweite Uraufführung der *Carmina Burana*"). Upon leaving Berlin for Munich, where he was living at the time, he made some dynamic modifications to the score that had occurred to him while listening to my performance.[5] I went to visit him, and he gave me a few loose pages on which he'd jotted down musical notations. He struck me as an incredibly sweet person, unmarred by any trace of the monstrous political movement with which historical critics so often associate him.

Looking Ahead

E VERYTHING I've recounted thus far contains the outlines of my many experiences, and the details of all I've learned, over the course of more than forty years spent with extraordinary orchestras and soloists who have given me suggestions, advice, habits, and philosophies I've held on to. I've traveled the world, which was an indispensable education in itself, as powerful as the journey of self-discovery undertaken by Goethe's Wilhelm Meister,[1] equally concrete and yet filled with the same unpredictable imaginative richness.

As my gaze shifted backward in time, I became worried that the past would remain a plain and mute melancholy, and I therefore felt the need to make something more of it, to tell others—especially the young musicians leaving the conservatory, freshly minted diplomas in hand—about my experience.

The many periods I spent preparing to bring a concert or opera to the public were filled with decisive moments that shaped my path and my reflections upon it. Sometimes they included "lessons" I led from the piano bench, for invariably large audiences, to elucidate the opera they'd be seeing two days later at La Scala; these lessons usually took place at Milan's various universities, and were regularly attended by a lot of students and opera enthusiasts. But in other cases—and these were the best opportunities—I was able to welcome audiences to our concert rehearsals, a phenomenon now referred to, in perhaps overly concrete terminology, as the "open rehearsal." There, although I behaved as usual with the orchestra, I tried to speak a bit more, to create a dialogue and involve the public, which always numbered in the hundreds. I really considered the public's presence, and tried to "open up" much more for them than just the theater doors! And so an ideal dialogue came about that has always intrigued me.

One afternoon at a theater in Prato, for instance—it must have been September 2006—I worked with the young musicians of the chamber orchestra on the beginning of Schubert's *Unfinished* Symphony. Holding the musicians' hands, first the cellists and double bass players and then the violinists, showing them how to produce the sound and, through it, visibly illustrate the miracle of the music's birth for the hundreds of people behind us was an unforgettable experience. It also satisfied a genuine need I felt: the need to communicate something, to break through, literally and metaphorically, the isolation that, for better or worse, the podium placed (and continues to place) me in.

It was a similar series of considerations that led me to dream of founding a youth orchestra. Considering the greatness of the musician, and my great love of his hometown Florence, I decided to name the ensemble after Luigi Cherubini. But when I left Milan and lost the underwriting by La Scala—no small thing, as you can imagine—the project fell into jeopardy for a little while. Luckily the Ravenna Festival and the theater of Piacenza were quick to get involved. We owe a lot to Piacenza's mayor and municipal culture councillor, and insofar as the ensemble is the "offspring" of the principal cities of both Emilia and Romagna, we perfectly represent the Emilia-Romagna region as a whole.

Finally the orchestra took shape. The city of Piacenza initially gave us the municipal theater, a marvelous home, soon supplemented by the newly restored Sala dei Teatini, where we now hold open rehearsals in the former church's transept and crossing, protected by a transparent acoustic chamber that improves the acoustics without obscuring the audience's view of the extensive frescoes. An international committee selects participants on an ongoing basis, because the statutes stipulate that musicians not stay on for more than three years or past the age of thirty (although a few of the musicians are allowed to come back as "adjuncts"). Therefore, rather than being a "competitive" orchestra, it is an "educational" orchestra. Membership isn't exclusively binding. That is, "dual citizenship" isn't prohibited: during their three-year tenure musicians are still allowed to participate in other courses and audition to join other ensembles. At the moment I'm working with the second group. We have won the Abbiati Prize, which is no small feat in a country as xenophilic as Italy. After hearing the orchestra perform in Ravenna at one of my concert-lessons on Beethoven's Fifth, the great director Jürgen Flimm, artistic director in Salzburg, invited the ensemble to take part in his festival program.

That occasion gave rise to the Neapolitan Project, an event organized to enliven the Salzburger Pfingstfestspiele (Pentecost Festival), which Karajan had virtually founded with his concerts in 1973. I had always tried to bring together a team that could resurrect the lesser-known musical pieces—and masterpieces—of the Neapolitan school, but the project had foundered in Italy. In Austria, however, we're already on our fourth year, and anyone who strolled the streets of Salzburg in May 2010 would have seen the ubiquitous posters with large letters that read *Neapel: Metropole der Erinnerung* ("Naples: The City of Memory," an amazing observation, although in the city of Naples itself no one has ever noticed!).

Today, as I continue the voyage that, with the works of Saverio Mercadante, will lead to the conclusion of the Neapolitan Project in Salzburg, it's worth looking back to when the whole idea was just a glimmer in my eye. I began to fall in love with the Neapolitan school in 1967, when Siciliani invited me to conduct a staging of Domenico Scarlatti's *La Dirindina* and Domenico Cimarosa's *Chi dell'altrui si veste presto si spoglia* at the Scarlatti Auditorium. Two of the period's greatest singers, Sesto Bruscantini and Paolo Montarsolo, played the lead parts, and Enriquez directed. Over time the seed began to germinate—beginning with the many hours I spent in the library at the Conservatory of San Pietro a Majella as a young student—and finally blossomed into the project carried out with Flimm.

In May 2010 the program focused on Mozart and Niccolò Jommelli. The orchestra played *Betulia liberata*, a work each composer had set to the libretto by Metastasio, and it made me unbelievably proud to see "my guys," all Italian musicians, perform Mozart in the very city that so jealously guards and celebrates his legacy. From one day to the next, they managed to perfectly produce two very distinct sounds—Mozart's classical and Jommelli's more old-fashioned. Considering that I knew Mozart's later masterpieces right up to *La clemenza di*

Tito inside out, I tended to think of *Betulia liberata*, a very early work done in 1771, as being an even earlier work of his juvenilia. But between the contribution of Jommelli, who was from Naples and of an older generation, and that of Mozart, who was from Salzburg and of a younger generation, there really was a noteworthy stylistic gap. The musicians of the Cherubini Orchestra understood that and gave the performance their all.

I was impressed that the fifteen-year-old Mozart could set such a complex text to music. Consider the interminable recitative at the beginning of the second act, which expatiates upon the nature of god with the rigor of an official theological debate—a passage that even the authors of the *Neue Mozart Ausgabe* suggested be trimmed. Mozart didn't miss a single apostrophe or accent. (In a letter written to his father around the time he was composing *Idomeneo*, he actually bragged, against his detractors' accusations, that he possessed a perfect knowledge of Italian and its prosody.) That has always been my credo: respect for the words of the libretto trumps abstract philology. Back in 1743, if the audience hadn't understood all the words, it would almost certainly have been bored with the work.

The Neapolitan Project will come to a close in 2011 with a rare opera by Mercadante, a composer deeply rooted in the Neapolitan school whose forward-looking work approaches that of Donizetti and Verdi. We'll revive *Li due Figaro*, based on a libretto by Felice Romani, with a score we tracked down in Madrid.

If I were asked to name some of the Cherubini Orchestra's particularly brilliant performances, they would include Paul Hindemith's *Sancta Susanna* in Ravenna in 2005, Shostakovich's

so-called *Dante* Sonatas, and the more recent performance of
Stravinsky's *Firebird Suite*. I've also done several tours with the
orchestra. A particularly memorable one took us to the Opéra
Garnier in Paris for five evenings, where we played Jommelli's
Demofoonte. When the work was presented, many people didn't
know who the composer was. I suggested they look upward as
they walked past the front of the opera house with the many busts
of famous musicians on its facade, and they'd see Jommelli's
name in gilt letters. I also held a series of classes with the same
young group of musicians, and each lesson was recorded and
made commercially available. I try to teach them two key things
above all: first, to have the dedication of a soloist while sitting
amid the rest of their section and pursuing the ideal of a unified
ensemble; second, to take an ethical approach to their profession.

The Cherubini Orchestra is also, as I mentioned, one of
Ravenna's orchestras, and in 2010 it participated alongside other
ensembles in the Viaggio dell'amicizia (Journey of Friendship),
an initiative that for several years now has been the most exciting
part of this festival that Cristina runs. Each year we've chosen
"martyr" cities, places where life is incredibly difficult, starting
with Sarajevo, which had just endured massive bombardments.
When I went there with the orchestra of La Scala, we traveled in
an Italian Air Force C-130, the plane usually used by paratroop-
ers. The Cherubini Orchestra played Schubert's *Gesang der
Geister über den Wassern* (Song of the Spirits over the Waters),
Brahms's *Schicksalslied* (Song of Destiny), and Beethoven's
Eroica Symphony. A major writer from Sarajevo thanked me in
an article published on the front page of the Italian newspaper
La Repubblica.

ABOVE LEFT: *Muti's mother, Gilda Muti Peli-Sellitto.*
ABOVE RIGHT: *Muti's father, Domenico Muti, in his second lieutenant medical corps uniform.*

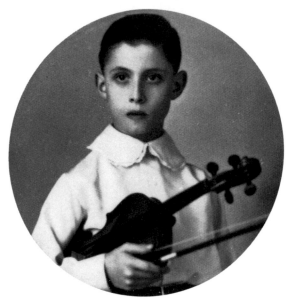

ABOVE: *Riccardo Muti's elementary school class; he is standing to the left of the teacher, his grandfather Donato.*

BELOW: *The young violinist in the early 1950s.*

OPPOSITE: *The young Muti playing the violin at a concert in Molfetta, May 15, 1952.*

Muti during an early rehearsal.

On break in his dressing room, age thirty.

M°. Riccardo Muti

OPPOSITE, TOP: *Conducting the Cantelli Competition award ceremony concert at the Teatro Coccia in Novara, 1967.*

OPPOSITE, BOTTOM: *An autographed portrait, 1968.*

ABOVE: *At the RAI Auditorium in Rome for the performance of Prokofiev's Third Symphony and Shostakovich's Thirteenth Symphony, 1969. The score of Shostakovich's Thirteenth, with lyrics by Yevtushenko, had been brought to Italy by Francesco Siciliani and translated into Italian. Muti is at far right, along with the first viola, Lodovico Coccon, and, in the background, the first cello, Giuseppe Selmi.*

ABOVE: *With his wife, Cristina, in the garden of their home in Ravenna, 1970s.*

BELOW: *With his son Domenico in 1979.*

OPPOSITE: *Walking through snowy Ravenna with his Boxer.*

With his children in his dressing room at La Scala, 1981.

At home with the family in Ravenna, 2000.

Cristina and Riccardo, 1980s.

ABOVE: *In Cortina d'Ampezzo, 1980s.*
BELOW: *At the Marina di Ravenna, 1980s.*

At the premiere of Antonio Salieri's L'Europa riconosciuta *on the occasion of La Scala's reopening, December 7, 2004.*

In the orchestra at La Scala.

During a concert at La Scala, 1990s.

Muti conducting (ABOVE) *and with director Giorgio Strehler* (BELOW) *in two photographs taken during rehearsals of* The Marriage of Figaro *at La Scala, 1982.*

Riccardo Muti
mit besonderem Dank und in
Bewunderung für seine gleichsam
zweite Uraufführung
der Carmina Burana
mit den Berliner Philharmonikern
am 25. VI. 1980

herzlichst

Carl Orff

OPPOSITE: *With Carl Orff in his dressing room* (ABOVE) *and onstage* (BELOW) *during the performance of* Carmina Burana *with the Berliner Philharmoniker, 1980.*
ABOVE: *An inscription from Carl Orff: "With particular thanks for your execution—a veritable second premiere—of* Carmina Burana *with the Berliner Philharmoniker," June 25, 1980.*

To Riccardo Muti with admiration and affection, Rudolf Serkin, January 1988

With Rudolf Serkin in Philadelphia, 1988.

With Vittorio Gui, founder of the Maggio Musicale Fiorentino festival, 1969 (ABOVE)*; composer Goffredo Petrassi watching a performance of his* Coro di Morti *at La Scala* (BELOW).

OPPOSITE: *On break with Luciano Pavarotti during the performance of Leoncavallo's* Pagliacci *in Philadelphia, 1992* (ABOVE); *with pianist Sviatoslav Richter in London, recording Beethoven's Third Concerto* (BELOW).
ABOVE: *With Eugene Ormandy, his predecessor as conductor of the Philadelphia Orchestra, 1970s.*

Al mio caro amico
e Maestro Riccardo
con la più profonda
amicizia riconoscenza
Gelu Kert 1978

OPPOSITE: *With soprano Renata Tebaldi, 1978* (ABOVE)*; with Jessye Norman in Philadelphia, 1980s* (BELOW).

ABOVE: *With his good friend Carlos Kleiber, in a photograph taken in Salzburg, 1995. Each signed the other's portrait.*

To Riccardo Muti, a great
artist and wonderful friend,
in sincere friendship
Claudio Arrau
1984.

*A photograph of Claudio Arrau, inscribed after a performance of
Beethoven's Fourth Concerto in Philadelphia, 1984.*

An inscribed photograph of Zino Francescatti, 1984.

An outdoor performance of Verdi's Messa da Requiem *in Busseto, with* the tenor Carlo Bergonzi.

ABOVE: *With the Philadelphia Orchestra, 1988.*
OVERLEAF: *After the first performance of* La Traviata *at La Scala in more than a quarter century, 1990.*

VIVA L

CONGRATULAZION

DEL TOURN

ARRIVE

On tour with the Filarmonica della Scala in Japan, 2003.

New Year's concert with the Wiener Philharmoniker, 1993.

With the Philharmonia Orchestra of London.

A concert with the Berliner Philharmoniker.

During the celebration of his 200th concert with the Wiener Philharmoniker at the Salzburg Festival, August 17, 2010.

With Pope John Paul II.

With Elizabeth II, queen of England, in his dressing room at La Scala, 2000 (before renovation).

During the Filarmonica della Scala's triumphant visit to Russia,
Riccardo and Cristina Muti with Mikhail and Raisa Gorbachev.

The Greatest

To Richard Muti –
"God has made you a messiah –
Your message is music, the
heartbeat of the universe."

"You are the greatest and so am I."

Peace

Muhammad Ali
May 10, 1986

An inscription from Muhammad Ali, May 10, 1986.

The 1995–96 season at La Scala, with some of the guest conductors Muti invited.

During a rehearsal with the Orchestra Giovanile Luigi Cherubini, a youth ensemble Muti founded.

The Chicago skyline.

Muti conducting the Chicago Symphony Orchestra.

Those trips were often adventurous and done in a highly limited time frame, and we certainly didn't do them in the spirit of "contractual observance" (to use a term that is sometimes a bit out of place). In July 2001 we performed the same concert twice, with just twenty-four hours in between, first in Erevan and then in Istanbul. We traveled to Turkey in an Armenian plane, creating an emotional bridge between two countries separated by a century of fighting and hatred.

In 2002 we played a memorial concert at New York's Avery Fisher Hall in Lincoln Center for the anniversary of the attack on the Twin Towers. Many people in the audience had lost someone, and held photos of them to their chests. After the concert some of them went downtown with me and the chorus of La Scala, where they sang "Va' pensiero" from *Nabucco* a cappella amid the chilling silence of Ground Zero.

Everywhere we go we ask local musicians to join us, right then and there (following a little advance preparation with one of their maestros), for a simple read-through so they can then play with us the evening of the concert. Many times the only thing musicians seated at the same stand have in common is the music, and yet they manage to express the same thing for two hours straight. I've found myself telling them, repeatedly, that a performance is a unifying, democratic act, a symbol of social congregation, in which you have to do your part without embarrassing those around you. Indeed, you have to work with your neighbor toward the "common good" (an often underrated ideal), especially when performing a quintessentially "social" form of music like a symphony.

Similarly, I've always thought there's nothing more didactic in a musician's schooling than the persistent and pedantic syllabification of the notes, which happens when solfeggio is poorly taught. That teaches the student to break the links between notes rather than sketch out a *continuous* musical path (which is ultimately the only true path) where the rhythm in no way obstructs the flow of the phrase. And solfeggio alone, it must be added, does not qualify as music or musical education. The process of learning music lies to a great extent in *listening* to music. And since it's far from obligatory, not to mention inconceivable, that we turn every child into a musician, our efforts would be best focused on teaching music appreciation. If you picture music as a forest of sounds, that would mean showing people the intricate paths that wind between the trees, connecting different kinds of sounds, and helping them experience it as a joyful place rather than a realm of cultural intimidation. Students could be familiarized, little by little, with the various instruments, greater and lesser musical forms, and the broader aesthetic aspects of themes. We could teach them to navigate that fascinating forest, just as a ten-month-old toddler is taught how to walk. I've tried to do exactly that, sometimes getting the public involved in rehearsal work and clarifying a piece's structure and most salient aspects in comprehensible yet serious terms. I've often had the satisfaction of seeing audience members' eyes light up, making them co-performers alongside me and the orchestra.

It's old news that nowadays all this is misunderstood, but I personally find the usual approach quite useless. In the best-case scenario it helps people learn to tickle the ivories, and maybe even play the piano fairly well, but it isn't a given that a proficient player is necessarily getting anywhere close to making music in a serious way. You can know how to play and still be worlds away.

Again, we shouldn't hope for squadrons of performers; rather, we should aim to create musicians and listeners capable of enjoying all the immense benefits that come from a real understanding of music. And to be honest, I even find the word "understanding" completely insufficient here, in music there's really very little to understand. For example, I myself and other professionals like me understand the form, harmony, counterpoint, color, tone, periods, and parentheses of a score, but all that's still just geometry, pure and simple. We'll never be able to entirely *understand* what's behind that framework—we can only hope to *feel* it, deep inside. So I'm very comfortable reassuring so-called musical incompetents. It's possible, and sometimes happens, that someone completely ignorant about musical form and language has a much deeper reaction to a piece than someone who, because he's performing it, has perforce to know the work inside out. The listener has evidently managed to more effectively "synthesize" the infinite messages the composer intended to convey. In the world of live music the pure, innocent neophyte is often worth more than the melomaniac or seasoned connoisseur trained by the hard, punitive practice of listening to albums.

Music's highly enigmatic nature distinguishes it from all the other arts. Everyone knows that its written "signs" are hopelessly inadequate, and for centuries people have tried in vain to capture and imprison the imponderable. Sometimes even we interpreters change from one evening to the next, either because we don't ultimately know what will happen or because our own point of view with regard to the masterpiece often isn't set in stone.

That's why one January afternoon in 1996, as I was rehearsing in Fiesole with the Orchestra giovanile italiana (Italian Youth

Orchestra), after a series of meticulous recommendations, I told the young musicians, "Watch out, tonight I might do something completely different from what I just did. What might that be? I myself don't even know!" It might be because of my aversion to the kind of performance that Theodor Adorno would call "reified," which I simply call "canned." In any case, they were surprised, were probably wondering what I was thinking, and may not even have understood. That afternoon I had noticed they were playing a bit too perfectly, too rigidly, as if their tuxes weighed as heavily on their shoulders as Gastone's.[2] I was growing increasingly impatient, and eventually a half-joke slipped out of my mouth: "We're Italians! Let's leave order to everyone else." By "everyone else" they probably thought I meant the Wiener or Berliner Philharmoniker! So much the better, for in a certain sense—taken *cum mica salis*, with a grain of salt—it was true. I remember reading an essay by Carmelo Bene in which Eduardo De Filippo is praised solely for his habit of changing some of the words he recited between the afternoon rehearsals and the evening performances. He even bragged about it—the ideal approach for any actor, including himself, he said, was to "complicate his life."[3] Maybe that time I wanted to complicate the lives of those young orchestra members.

And anyway, anybody can understand that in the music profession you can change, you can switch things up—you have to improvise sometimes, and you can never count on any given passage coming out identically from one performance to the next. Take the beginning of Mozart's Symphony in G Minor: it's one of the most difficult attacks imaginable, not because of its famous "tune," which any audience member could hum along with when it parallels the accompaniment, but because of that first measure of *only* accompaniment. You're probably thinking, that's easy, it happens all the time, even in arias like "La Donna è mobile" or "Di Provenza il mare, il suol." But here the sheer surge of the music is dizzying, and a line of violas has to start out from the silence alone, with a movement forced to *immediately* create the anxious atmosphere leading up to that fantastic "tune." I said "leading up to," but there's no time. Everything has to happen in an instant. A few music historians have wondered why Mozart didn't write a few more anticipatory bars or start in directly with the rise of the theme. He didn't precisely because he's Mozart and he wanted to give the tension an all-consuming power by condensing it into an incredibly short time span—an instant forced to come to terms with the infinite, so the only thing you can say is that there are no words for it. In reality, that first bar can end up a disaster. You have to consider the hall, its character, the viola players and the mood they're in, whether they'll all be in the right frame of mind for those notes.

That's more or less what I ended up saying to the bass player during rehearsals of Mozart's *Vesperae solennes de confessore* in Florence in March 2006, just before we began playing "Laudate Dominum." I couldn't not warn him that the F he had to begin on would be the most difficult note of his life. I even added, "I wouldn't want to be in your shoes." Then—and I can still see this—I asked him to "find a quivering deep within yourself," and to clarify what I meant I recommended, "Play in such a way that this first note is—" and I made the gesture of lightly blowing something into the air off the palm of my hand. He cracked a good-humored smile. He wasn't afraid in the least, and it really didn't look like this was the most serious moment of his life. But I was trying to make him see that the silence before the sound has to be charged with a singular energy that is then released into the sound, as if the music had begun before the instruments had even emitted that first note. The conductor, viola players, and bass player are completely absorbed, not because they're racking their brains about the tempo to take off with, but rather because they're looking deep within themselves to observe the expressive content that they'll have to make perceptible to the public an instant later. I can't explain it any better, and that's why I'm always amazed at the boldness with which some conductors dive into their music, producing something that may be well done but upon closer examination has more to do with mechanical order than with any emotional suggestion.

It's these aspects that distinguish one player from the next, and in musical training I find few things more useful than comparing different interpretations of the same piece. That's one of the priceless advantages recorded albums give us, and I'm certain that, when it comes to aiding musical comprehension, they produce much more substantial results than handing a kid a recorder and seeing what improbable sounds he'll get from it.

Of course, all the elements I've tried to explain just now are impossible to quantify, and none of us can ever say for sure whether a given interpreter is conscientious and serious, as if saying to himself, "Now I'll step up to the podium and do it this way."

Many times I've found myself somehow "different," without knowing what was happening or how. I remember one evening in particular, when I was conducting the Adagio from

Bruckner's Seventh Symphony with the Wiener Philharmoniker. At one point during the "normal" execution of the work I noticed that something magical was happening. It's just an instant, a "something" that doesn't last long and seems to depend less on you than on a series of circumstances accompanied by a wave of emotion whose source you can't quite distinguish: Is it the orchestra? The audience? You? You don't know, but you feel it, and it seems like an apparition. Alas, at the very moment you realize that something larger than anything you're capable of producing has been born, well, the miracle slips through your fingers. I recently picked up again a book that speaks of this exact phenomenon.[4] It talks about Stendhal's comments, in *Racine and Shakespeare*, on theatergoers and their reactions while watching a performance. Stendhal thinks no viewer can ever really identify with a play for its entire duration—two or three hours, say—but instead identifies with it only in a few privileged moments, when he really loses himself and miraculously becomes a part of the play, feeling it in his body and soul. He calls these few seconds "the moment of perfect illusion." And Stendhal is convinced that it's worth going to the theater just for that sole moment.

Obviously, it starts with good execution—if that's missing you can't expect any miracles—and then, if you're lucky, the orchestra becomes a single entity, everyone senses something is about to happen, and there isn't even one distracted musician thinking about something else; such is the magnetic power of "identification"! A transcendent internal energy is created, and you the conductor are the first to become an innocent, incredulous, ecstatic spectator. You can't plan it. If one evening, after the houselights have gone down, you stand before the orchestra about to conduct *Manon Lescaut* and say to yourself, "Tonight I want to do better than ever before," you can bet that will be the worst performance. Reason cannot inform feeling, and the paths connecting the two realms are invariably inscrutable.

I have to believe that this is how it really is, both for me—and I've lived on music for the past fifty years—and for all the enthusiasts lost out there in the audience. There are certain simple, chance moments in life that have reminded me of this mysterious aspect of music in an indelible way. One evening in 1999 I was conducting Verdi's *Requiem* in Jerusalem, in a place called the Sultan's Pool, just outside the ancient walls of Zion. As usual, I didn't stop for intermission, pausing only briefly before the Offertory. The silence was pierced by a cry that must have been the whine of a dog or some other animal, and it seemed to come from the nearby desert. I prolonged the pause, waiting for the lament to end. There, before the walls of Jerusalem, it sounded like a voice directly linked to all creation and the world of the Old Testament. But because the break risked running too long—we were being broadcast live and had to respect the television schedule—I decided to proceed anyway, attacking the cellos' introduction to the Offertory. Like a charm, as soon as the music began, the howling ceased. It was as if that distant voice had risen up to ask us not to stop the music, and fell silent only when the magical song returned.

Another time, in 2005, we were in the Tunisian desert town of El Jem, and I was conducting the Maggio Musicale ensemble in selections from Arrigo Boito's *Mefistofele*. Just as one piece ended and we prepared to begin another, the prayer call of a muezzin rose up from a distant mosque. At first the audience, the orchestra, the chorus, the soloists, and I myself were all dumbfounded at the unexpected "intrusion." But then I realized that, to my ears, that spiritual call sounded almost as if it were an innate part the opera's atmosphere. It mirrored it, giving it a connective tissue of sorts that, far from being intrusive, actually heightened its depth. So I let the call finish before I began. When it ended the Tunisian audience burst into loud applause to thank me for the respect I'd shown, and the music continued with even greater intensity. Such are the miracles that song—be it the call of a muezzin or a page of Boito—creates!

CHAPTER ELEVEN

Music Is Limitless

TODAY, the final test of my artistic life will be my collaboration with the Chicago Symphony Orchestra. I thought I was
done with America after my extended stay in Philadelphia, but in
February 2010 I returned to work with the Metropolitan Opera,
a felicitous occasion. James Levine had invited me several times
before, but my work with La Scala was so absorbing that, despite
my desire to go, I always had to say no. So I finally went and
conducted *Attila*, and it was a fantastic experience because of
the high-level artistry of both orchestra and chorus. And they
showed me such warmth: At the end of each performance the
musicians stayed in the pit for the length of the applause, clapping along with the rest of the audience; the chorus members
came to my dressing room and gave me a pair of cufflinks
engraved "Attila 2010—Metropolitan Chorus"; and the technicians brought me as a souvenir a miniature Odabella,[1] costume
and all, which they had made by copying a Barbie doll.

And now Chicago, a surprising new encounter—surprising for me even more than anyone else. President Deborah
Rutter had contacted me more than once when she was looking for a new music director. First she persuaded me to conduct
a concert. I hadn't been to Chicago in about thirty years, and

my initial meeting with the orchestra revealed such an intense understanding between us that in 2008 I led them on a European tour. Situations like that make it clear whether the relationship between conductor and orchestra is destined to fall apart or grow even stronger. Some of them wrote to me afterward about how happy they were with the experience, and the invitations from the president and board grew more insistent.

I hesitated for a long while. I had actually decided, following my years at La Scala, that I was ready to take more time for myself. This might sound naïve, but I had always had little time to myself, and now—as Seneca famously wrote in one of his letters—even an enormous tree that wasn't yet a meter high when I planted it in my garden was standing there like a mirror, showing me the very image of time passing, *my* time.[2] That's just it, "Who can catch the passing years?"[3]

In the end, however, their warm invitation and my insatiable curiosity for future projects induced me to accept. There was one condition I had already mentioned to the board: at this age, just making music—even exquisite music—wouldn't be enough for me. I wanted to do everything in my power to bring it to social classes that, for various reasons entirely beyond their control or active choice, are excluded from this kind of culture. I planned to do so even if it meant "decentralizing" the performances, and leaving Symphony Center. Chicago is a very multiethnic city, with vastly different layers, many of which are completely unfamiliar with the classical music tradition. I was especially thinking of the U.S. prison system and its juvenile detention centers, where so many kids are doing time. I consulted the great cellist Yo-Yo Ma, who wholeheartedly agreed with me, and we've

already set some dates when we'll bring music into the peniten-
tiaries—either as a duet with me at the piano or with a smaller
version of the Chicago Symphony Orchestra.

This won't be an entirely new experience for me. A few
months ago I performed in the Bollate prison in Milan. I was
officially invited by Lucia Castellano, the institution's enlightened director (who is also originally from Naples), but the idea
had first come from one of the inmates, who had written me a
letter. Some 150 prisoners sat on the steps of a small amphithe-
ater and listened to me play Beethoven, Schubert, and Chopin
on the piano. The situation highlighted a terrible contrast: on
the one hand was the music, which by its very nature alludes
to a better world, and on the other there were the shadows of
the crimes that had led to the inmates' imprisonment. But there
was also music's ability to console. It reminded me of the entry
in *Last Letters from Stalingrad* that describes an army officer, in
December 1942, playing the *Appassionata* on a piano out in the
street. "Those hundred recruits sat there cloaked, their blankets
pulled up over their heads. You could hear shooting everywhere,
but no one was distracted: they were listening to Beethoven in
Stalingrad."[4] And I told them all that even those notes were the
creative result of often unhappy souls. That supremely memorable evening made me reflect that a maestro shouldn't seek out
the limelight. Especially in the latter part of his life, once he's
had a career, he should withdraw from the media and try, as
much as possible, to bring music to others so that he, ephemeral
himself, doesn't fall victim to the ephemeral nature of conducting. After all, we aren't creators, only "translators," and therefore we never leave anything definitive behind us, because the

criteria and tastes of musical interpretation change with time.

Bollate wasn't Poggioreale,[5] but everything surrounding it was slightly intimidating—even the black cars with "Penitentiary Police" painted on their sides that took us there—and made me view that world, so different from ours, with great diffidence. We entered through a huge iron gate, which gave me the shivers. But as soon as we were inside I saw workshops where the inmates made ornaments to brighten the place, and I understood that, despite the weight of their sentences, there was a real attempt at rehabilitation.

In the hall where I played, men and women, dressed with great care, looked like the best audience possible, and I spoke to them as if we weren't surrounded by bars. I was so caught up in the conversation that I pointed to one of the men and asked (using the formal *lei*), "Where are you from?"—a question that always comes out spontaneously, even when I meet young singers for the first time, I don't really know why, maybe to determine my behavior by gauging their answer. You'll never believe this, but he replied, "From Molfetta." For a few seconds I was left "as one who suddenly before him sees something whereat he marvels." That is, if I remember correctly from my high school literature class, I had the same reaction Sordello had upon seeing Virgil, a fellow Mantuan: "O pride eternal of the place I came from"![6] Then I tested him by saying a couple of sentences in dialect, and he understood perfectly.

I'd chosen works that weren't too complex, and began with Schumann's "Warum?" (Why?). All of us, over the course of our lives, ask millions of questions, many of which will never be answered, and I felt no one could understand that better than they. I continued with some Chopin preludes, short pieces—of a dodecaphonic brevity—that could grab the audience, even if they were a bit modern. I explained that Hans von Bülow managed to give each one a title, translating all of its expressive content into a single word. A Schubert impromptu made them smile because I told them about that old film about him, with the scene where he's with his bohemian friends and mentions that he's fallen in love. When asked who his sweetheart is, he sits down at the piano to play that sublimely poetic piece.[7] His friends' reactions are pretty hammy: the cigar falls from one guy's mouth; the painter's brush stops in its tracks; they're all rather thunderstruck. In the end, the musician reveals her name.

I ended the performance by recounting something of Beethoven's life and his battle against physical and spiritual suffering, and then played the *Moonlight* Sonata. They unanimously felt that was the most beautiful piece of the whole concert. That was one of the most singular evenings of my life. They came up afterward to have their pictures taken, and I was surrounded by a marvelous humanity.

*

One day in my high school philosophy class the great teacher Domenico De Simone read us a line from Nietzsche. I fell in love with it, and it has often helped those who, like me, find themselves traveling the world with a "nest of memories" in their hearts: "It is not a matter of missing the past, but rather of realizing its potential." My experience at Bollate—like all the most serious experiences of my life—lives on in my mind not as a simple memory or impotent nostalgia, but as an event whose potential I now have to realize. It's an event that also casts some light on what I *will* do over the next few years in Chicago.

Il duolo e la bell'anima:
Sorrow and the Noble Soul
by Marco Grondona

To debate whether music has meaning and content is not particularly worthwhile; it is much better to assume that it does and go from there. In any case, that assumption is automatic when you see Muti conduct, after a piece by Verdi, Schubert's *Great*.[1] You get the impression, reinforced by his gestures, that you are watching invisible characters, conjured from the music stands, who converse with and recognize one another. (He often raises his hand to his ear, signaling the various "classes" to listen to one another.) To paraphrase Artaud, "the eye is as moved as the ear." Muti's aptitude for creating veritable "theater"—not only with *Tosca* and *La Traviata* but with all symphonies—allows the audience to identify with the work, even with a severe instrumental work like Haydn's *Seven Last Words of Christ,* in which there are passages that can be "more human and more moving than they are symphonic":[2]

At the beginning of Mozart's *Vesperae*, when the chorus musters truly genuine enthusiasm to proclaim "iuravit Dominus et non poenitebit eum," his best advice to the orchestra is "Never think symphonically!":[3]

In Schubert's *Scherzo* the dance's rallentandos and rubato save it from the miserable practice of *herunterspielen*, the "downplaying" that Wagner detested in the conductors of his period—a charge that Adorno even made against Toscanini.[4] *Apotheose des Tanzes*: "One cannot play a dance piece without dancing in one way or another," I once heard Muti say to the Orchestra del Maggio when it was guilty of being overly dignified. And when conducting the young musicians of the Cherubini Orchestra as they played Schubert, he asked for "something fit for a New Year's Concert!"

In the final section of the *William Tell* Overture, with the *galop*, he stubbornly prevented the strings from daring to take even a minuscule breath between the half phrases,

which ended up almost moving those subphrases (also known as *incisi*, or musical incises) closer, *stringendo* to the point of ending on the sixteenth notes and beginning the tune all over again from the eighth note on a downbeat.[5] Obviously, this was a mere split-second impression, but in this way the phrase was transformed and miraculously *à bout de souffle*. Going from the E major to the bars in C-sharp minor, the difficulty becomes paroxysmal:[6]

The maestro was convinced—I believe—that taking another breath would almost involuntarily set the piece up to "sing" and therefore tarnish the proud, strong rhythm, which just then had to exert its radical nature. Otherwise "it becomes *cantabile* (singable), and the rhythmic sense is lost."[7] (I had the sensation—and I consider this a blessing when at the theater—that each evening the metronome was quicker than the last!) The same was true of the symphony in *La forza del destino*—especially when I heard it as a concert overture that tore through the entire plot in just ten minutes. In the second section, Andantino, the woodwinds tell of "le minacce, i fieri accenti" (the threats, the proud accents) and the first violins very freely stretch out the "destiny" theme (that is, the one the "symphonic poem" began with):

And^te con espressione

Reading *senza tempo* (without tempo) here evokes the desperate voice of breathlessness, and there is an urge to "drag"—lingering on the sigh that ends the second minor, which, for tonal reasons, is also the "interval of the heart"[8]—as only Mahler's pitiful *schleppend* can. The maestro treated the signature theme of Nina's astonishment at the finale of Paisiello's drama *Nina, ossia La pazza per amore* the same way, and said, "It's a heartbeat—almost *free.*"

Note, and this is not an exaggeration on my part, how much a maxim of that sort might sound like an oxymoron: it is widely accepted that, according to Riemann's famous definition, the quality of the rhythm depends precisely on "determining the correct tempo—which governs the rhythm of a musical piece—based on the average normal pulse of a healthy person,"[9] while reference works explain that "the system of musical tempos evidently originates in the human organism and, in particular, refers to the rhythm of a medium-speed pulse (more or less between 60 and 80 beats per minute). This gives rise to the categorical perceptions *lento* and *allegro* as possible products of a musical movement,"[10] and "all widespread theories, from all periods, that postulate a necessary relationship between tempo and certain biological functions—like pulse and heartbeat and walking speed—share the idea of an average tempo that serves as reference point."[11] The fact that for Muti the pulse, that presumed paradigm of "measure," becomes the model for setting a "tempo *a piacere*" (literally "tempo at pleasure," or "as you please") illustrates his style—in just two words, and much better than any lengthy explanation of mine ever could.

One day I heard him say: "I've been thinking about the symphony from *Norma* for a long time now. Someday I might like to do it in an entirely different way—maestoso." And then he began slowly singing the beginning, giving the chords a touch of vibrato, the nobility of a choral piece, somehow transforming Bellini's Allegro maestoso e deciso into a tempo that was simply Maestoso or perhaps even Grave e maestoso (the German equivalent, a one-word, commonly used term, would be Feierlich):

All° Maestoso e Deciso

I think the maestro felt a need and a desire for a more serious beginning (a *tempo primo* of sorts,[12] bars 1–14? 1–34?), free of the tempo *alla bersagliera* (energetic, "fast and furious") that is its fatal flaw from the attack onward in all contemporary interpretations. Especially because—according to the "text"—the same movement has to be maintained throughout, from start to finish (indeed, the score does not include any changes in tempo). Muti must have considered it one of those cases in which *littera enim occidit spiritus autem vivificat*.[13] He must have felt it was the perfect occasion to shake off courageously any and every "authoritarian foundation."[14] That, in turn, reminds me of one of the more fascinating questions surrounding Wagner's approach to conducting (Wagner, of course, was a famous orchestra conductor at a young age and for at least a century remained an influential model for future generations): which tempo to use in the overture of Gluck's *Iphigénie en Aulide*. The main concern expressed in his 1854 essay is that it not be rushed from bar 19 on (out of habit, as a consequence of the Largo-Allegro overture), preserving the initial Andante throughout the piece (according to the "text") in order to avoid the "vulgar noise" that was part and parcel of German conductors' practice,[15] and thereby guarantee that the first theme has a unified sound of "massive breadth" (*maßive Breite*):[16]

Muti conducts Bellini's symphony quite brilliantly from the very first measure, and he uses a tempo that is markedly more allegro than that employed by any other conductor.[17] But even here I must make one "dramatic" clarification: I heard Muti's quite rapid execution during the encore of a concert,[18] and in that mode the piece was truly revolutionized. It was transformed from its original role (as a prelude to the drama) and became a complete action in and of itself, *illico et immediate*—and credit is due to the maestro for having so precisely conveyed the change! The time he joined a real band (not Hans Werner Henze's ideal "band"!)[19] in Ravenna to play the lively overture on June 14, 2008, was equally fascinating.[20] It is no coincidence that the maestro's "first music-related memory" is of the local bands in Molfetta ("day and night, a slow, dramatic music" when "the local band emphatically launched into the most famous local funeral march"),[21] and the infallible Fedele D'Amico reminds us that, because Verdi's creativity with timbre was ablaze even in his very first operas, "the opinions against him arose both from the disgust many people felt at anything echoing the glory of local bands as well as from the fact that his tones are often juxtaposed rather rudimentarily."[22] Muti always had the good sense to eschew such disgust.

So a certain amount of violence and, obviously, tragedy was certainly present in the symphony of *La forza del Destino*. The two themes were no longer just music, but actually appeared to be *personae*—dramatic characters in their own right—and the relationship between them, entirely free with regard to tempo, transformed the "awkwardness" Budden so disliked into one gigantic effect.[23] Something similar occurred in another passage from the symphony of *Norma*—again, when he performed it in isolation as an encore, when everyone is expecting miracles and oversized, amazing feats. The brief symphonic poem's theme is well known. As usual, in addition to the new material he presented a few elements drawn from the music of the opera. This not only gave the audience the pleasure of recognizing a bit two hours after they'd heard it the first time around, after the curtains rose, but also allowed him to create a new "plot" that wasn't just a slavish imitation. In this case, the most evidently singable episode was

an extended fragment of the last, desperate duet: Norma is radiant upon seeing that Pollione—at the thought of Adalgisa con-
demned to burn at the stake—is finally as unhappy as she herself
is ("Già mi pasco ne' tuoi sguardi, del tuo duol, del suo morire":
Already, in your eyes, I feed upon your anguish for her death):

Even a viewer who knew nothing of the tragedy about to unfold
would have had a strong feeling of what was about to happen,
because Muti chose to bring back the lower of the two voices, producing a song—if you'll allow me to use an obsolete term that really
applies here—marked by uncontrolled "alienation" and led by the
piccolo as if it had strayed from the ranks of a coarse band, *con voce
nudrita*,[24] "all brusque and robust, *molto vivace, senza complimenti*,
the sound that so often enchants us in Bellini in front of his band":[25]

In short: in both melodrama and spoken theater, one can perform
absolute music and start the "drama" right at the very beginning—as Wagner was enamored of doing—in the symphonic
introduction.

In Rossini's *Moïse*, for example, the introduction is certainly the most subtle piece that approaches *Nabucco*, but the

"choral" that is so clear in Verdi is instead hidden behind a superior bravura in Rossini:

because he omitted the form's characteristic legato and wrote brief notes, separating them and setting pauses between them (the exact opposite of more traditional choral works). It ends up sounding more futuristic and "unheimlich," worthy of inclusion in the composer's catalogue of late piano works. (At the time, a similar sound could be found only in the second movement of Beethoven's op. 14 no. 2, the *Spring* Sonata, or in the Allegretto movement of his *Moonlight* Sonata, with its forced accents and bizarre placement of the pauses):

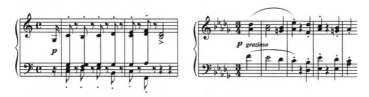

I have heard this kind of styling—the kind of emotional, dramatic but also slightly spirited touch that immediately jumps out from the written score—*only* in the performance of the Filarmonica della Scala when they performed at the Teatro degli Arcimboldi, where, with ingenious violence, the instruments showered the abstract choral part with sonorous flashes and little fires.

The ability to light up minute subphrases in an "uninformed phrase sketched out with lightning-like speed"[26] results in one of the miracles Maestro Muti performs in the theater: the violins that introduce the scene and Lindoro's aria in Paisiello's *Nina*, for example, hold the G note for three measures, then an interminable D for another three (the tonic and dominant hence adjusting themselves), but in between lies an unnoticed sub-phrase of just three eighth-notes, a scale fragment:

and for Muti that is what must become the "Song." He stops, and points it out to the innocently unaware orchestra: "It's a melodic event!" (beyond very slow grace notes). His observation is spot-on. While it's clear that, for the G major of the aria, the E makes up for the "interval of the heart," the maestro's instinct—which gave rise to the quoted section—is ultimately what correctly iso-lates a tune that, merely in terms of duration, has a relationship of 3:26 with its surrounding context! And then, seeing a con-tinuation of certain parts' roles in the score (the sixth of the E resolves on the fifth of the D), leads to an even greater apprecia-tion of his solution (the well and truly isolated subphrase). The same feeling is evoked at the beginning of the finale of the first act. It saves the sixth interval, much as happens in a theme from Haydn's Sonata no. 6, where he begs the first violins to hold the note "as if you didn't want to leave it behind":

Close inspection reveals that Muti has made a veritable treasure of the grace notes that press on toward that G with an irresistible lyric urgency. This same sensibility inspired Wagner's authentic passion for the oboe's little cadence in the first movement of Beethoven's Fifth; he wrote about it in *Über das Dirigiren* and confessed that, as a conductor, he had come to understand the whole symphony only once he was capable of "singing" that measure:

> A long time ago I derived much instruction as to the tempo and the proper execution of Beethoven's music from the clearly accentuated, expressive singing of the great Ms. Schröder-Devrient. I have since found it impossible, for example, to allow the touching cadence of the oboe in the first movement of the Fifth Symphony to be played in the customary timid and embarrassed way; indeed, beginning with the insight I had gained into the proper execution of this cadence, I also found and felt the true significance and expression due to the sustained fermata of the first violins in bar 22. Thus, from the touching emotional impressions I got by means of these two seemingly insignificant details, I gained a new point of view, from which the entire movement appeared in a clearer, warmer light.[27]

So, can it be a coincidence that for exactly two themes in *The Seven Last Words of Christ* with grace notes:

Muti presses the members of the orchestra? For the first, he asks them to execute it "without anyone interrupting, and without doing it in fits and starts: otherwise, as you can hear, it immediately turns into a dance!"[28] and for the second he dispenses a simple yet resolute piece of advice: "Sure, it might be a group of grace notes, but you must always think of it as a melodic event, not just a group of grace notes."[29] This clearly goes back to the sublime fantasies of *Dirigiren*, transforming what at first glance seemed to be an insignificant detail into pure "song."[30] The proof can be found on a dense page of the *Vesperae solennes* where, between orchestra and chorus, the grace notes dominate the melodies:[31]

I cannot help but reference the brief symphonic poem in the prologue of Wagner's *Götterdämmerung* when, after the Norns have vanished, *the glow of daybreak grows ever brighter, and the flicker of firelight in the background grows ever dimmer*, just before

Siegfried and Brünnhilde emerge from the room carved into the
face of the cliff:[32]

This time, Muti relates a bona fide apologue to the musicians
and chorus. He stops and puts their backs against the wall with
special urgency: "Bravo, sure, go ahead and do it like that! But

when you go to conduct the beginning of K. 550, what will you
tell them? How will you explain it?" I will try to translate this in
my own very humble prose: the alto and soprano violins of the
Vesperae, executing the grace notes *a strascìno* (dragging them
out) and tossing them away, risk misunderstanding their lyri-
cism (in a technical sense, the possibility of making them "sing")
and, therefore, when facing the famous beginning of a masterpiece such as Mozart's Symphony in G Minor, they would be the
first to turn it into the kind of insufferable charivari that virtually
all conductors reduce it to. I'm referring, of course, to conductors who do not understand just how much *melos* even the Molto
allegro and the series of seconds in K. 550 can contain! Muti uses
this charming comparison to exhort the musicians—not for the
first or last time—to *sing* with their instruments. Perhaps deep
down he is convinced that Sylvie Vartan was not entirely mis-
taken in turning this piece into a love song, using it for "Questa
musica vibra nell'aria / e racchiude una grande magia, / mi
trascina in un mondo incantato / dove regna la tua fantasia"
(This music vibrates in the air / and envelops a great magic, /
sweeping me away into an enchanted world / where your imagination reigns."[33] "The Mozart melody," Gino Stefani wrote, "is,
as everyone can hear, readily singable. . . . That song was the
final step in the popular reduction of the tune, adding words and
vocally appropriating it. Well, it was a singable tune, right? And
so by singing it, she ultimately returned it to its ideal, original
condition."[34] Furthermore, what happened during the rehearsal
of the *Vesperae* points out something else: the maestro, enamored of song, sees the grace notes as an emblem, just as young
Richard Wagner (who, as already noted, first found fame as an

extraordinary orchestra conductor) did. This is not an "old" example, but it is a renowned one. Today it comes in handy as it distinguishes Muti from those music theorist Heinrich Schenker called—with more than a hint of bitterness tinged with disdain—"die jungen Dirigenten,"[35] those young conductors, who, on principle, refuse to "sing" even the refrain of "La donna è mobile."

"As if you didn't want to leave it behind" has also been, since Wagner's day, a true rule for those who play in an orchestra. Allow me to cite another passage from the *Vesperae*[36] that also begins "like a dance." In this passage, Muti is most concerned that the musicians "not lose the sonorous tension of the long note!":

As Wagner writes in *Über das Dirigiren*, "Our orchestras nowadays hardly know what is meant by *equally sustained tone*. Let any conductor ask any orchestral instrument, no matter which,

for a full and prolonged forte, and he will find the player puzzled, and will be astonished at the trouble it takes to get what
he asks for."[37] And so, the maestro laments to the soprano who
in Gluck's *Iphigénie en Aulide* was supposed to be just *une autre
femme grecque* in the fifth scene of the first act, "Signora: 'guè-è-
è-èrre.' The note has to be long! Long and even!" After a pause,
he adds, "This is one of the new generation's defects [it tends to
let the sound go], even in the orchestra!"

This passion for *one* note is not just for purposes of safe-
guarding a sound technique that risks being overwhelmed by
superficiality (as Wagner saw it). It is also a sign of supreme control over details that—contrary to appearances—does not pre-
clude the "whole"; rather, especially in theater, it makes *everything* capable of representative expression and subject to pathos.
To take just one example, from the final thirty measures of *Moïse*,
consider the magnificent "ocean calm" that translates Beethoven
and Schubert into the "Italian style," but also "the deathly, terrible quiet" of Goethe's poem *Meeresstille* (Quiet Sea). Muti
must have grasped what Rossini was aiming for with that final
C major chord: to whisper dying Socrates' final sentence into
the audience's ear—"Crito, we owe a cock to Asclepius. But
you pay up and don't fail to take care." There is even a hint of

Nietzsche when he exclaims, to our dismay: "He who has ears, hear—oh Crito, life is but a delusion":[38]

For the first time, listening to Muti, I saw the double descending tetrachord on the score that—alas, toward the very end—precedes the resplendent C (a *basso di lamento* naturally written in C minor:[39] C, B-flat, A-flat, G) so that the final calm has something of the libertine's dismal contentment, of Schumann's unresolved question *Warum?*—"And now?"[40]

The march of the Hebrews in the first act arrives "from a distance" and strongly conjures up offstage action, an effect that has been part of music history since the eighteenth century (the gradual crescendo and diminuendo of someone coming close and then slowly disappearing). That evening, it was reborn with all the strength of a bona fide *Ritirata notturna di Madrid*.[41] This is one of the maestro's special touches. Years ago, he used it to point out the identical "situation" in a diabolical passage from *The Marriage of Figaro*—unsettling for critics, normally overlooked in the orchestra and therefore completely invisible to the audience (the finale of act 3: "Ecco la marcia, andiamo"):

The commentary reflected people's astonishment: the "truly curious wedding march, which has something rigid and contracted about it, something acidic,"[42] "produces an almost alienating effect, like a march of tin soldiers."[43]

Muti simply "made scenic" a piece of music that generally is not:[44] even if he has not read Bekker's *Story of the Orchestra*—and there's no knowing whether he has—he marvelously realized its postulate[45] with his instinctive way of being absorbed and getting lost in the score. Just as Adorno, in ten wise, well-interpreted lines, provided an infallible criterion to all those who, for better or worse, are forced to make music: if you want to interpret a line of music, stop reflecting; your only option is to "copy it." In a slightly over-the-top paragraph in *Music and Language: A Fragment*, Adorno wrote:

> To interpret language means: to understand language. To interpret music means: to make music. Musical interpretation is performance, which, as synthesis, retains the similarity to language, while obliterating every specific resemblance. This is why the idea of interpretation is not an accidental attribute of music, but an integral part of it. To play music correctly means first and foremost to speak its language properly. This calls for imitation of itself, not a deciphering process. Music only discloses itself in mimetic practice, which admittedly may take place silently in the

imagination, in an analogy with silent reading; it never yields to a scrutiny that would interpret it independently of fulfillment. If we were to search for a comparable act in the languages of intention, it would have to be the act of transcribing a text [*abschreiben*], rather than decoding its meaning.⁴⁶

This, in my very humble opinion, is Muti's distinctive quality, the thing that makes him say, at the beginning of the second act of *Nina*, "there's no need for road signs; certain things are implicit in the music." It is also what makes him different from everyone who occasionally cares about "keeping their distance from the execution" (like—just to be absolutely clear—all the times a heavyweight conductor such as Carlos Kleiber "unabhängig von ihrem Vollzug deutet"!).⁴⁷ Therefore, in order to indicate how the stylistic formula had become overly manifest in Susanna's aria "Per l'amata padroncina"—and therefore the uselessness, at that moment, of Muti's role as the person "keeping the beat"⁴⁸—he suggested to the orchestra: "Do it naturally, in whatever way it spontaneously comes to you":

Toscanini evoked the same idea. "Many times," he confessed to Adriano Lualdi, "I feel that it is the chorus, the orchestra that need to sing; and so, without them even realizing it, I abandon them just a bit to their healthy instincts and the sacred enthusiasm of the moment, and it is I who follow them."⁴⁹

On the contrary, in *The Marriage of Figaro*, at the beginning of the fourth act, the old-fashioned "formula" is only an appearance (even if Paisiello is quoted by Hermann Abert). "L'ho perduta, me meschina" (I have lost it, woe is me) represents the climax of an unspeakable void:

Indeed, I cannot help but think that Barbarina's pathetic lament is a close relative of Cecchina's "Vo cercando e non ritrovo la mia pace, il mio conforto" (I am looking and yet cannot find peace, consolation) in the beginning of the finale of *Buona figliola* (Piccinni, 1760). Like the great Russian director Stanislavski, Muti interrupts rehearsals, in this case to suggest that the soprano fully absorb the situation: "Signora, you haven't merely lost a brooch; not even you realize what you have lost." Similarly, Stanislavski once counseled a student at his school thusly:

> No, do not try to make us believe that the first time you were looking for the pin.. . . You did not even think of it. You merely sought to suffer, for the sake of suffering.
>
> But the second time you really did look. We all saw it; we understood, we believed, because your consternation and distraction actually existed.
>
> Your first search was bad. The second was good.[50]

And in the opera's finale, with abrupt changes in tempo and tone, the ensembles' performance gains substance—with Lento and Allegro it sharply replicates astonishment and discomfiture—without running any risk of repeating itself, because all the episodes come together under the umbrella of an agogic indication: *Religioso*. This just seems right. It feels like the only way to label in no uncertain terms the substantial, scabrous analogy between the Contessa's body and the *verum corpus* of the last motet.[51]

In fact, this offers the surprise of a new "sound." In *The Seven Last Words of Christ*, he considered the last sonata, "In manus tuas, Domine," "the strangest, most abstruse piece," so before beginning he employed the best technique available to get the orchestra on the same page with him: he didn't open his mouth, but rather stooped down and hummed the initial "motto":[52]

It was one of those irrevocable gestures,

taking song as the point of departure: the way everyone from Mariani to Mancinelli, Toscanini, and Serafin has always done it, and the way the best orchestra conductors still do it today; because, in terns of efficacy and precision, no means can equal that of *singing* a phrase, a cue, a simple subphrase aimed at the stage artist or orchestral performer to help them understand, by offering *the model to imitate*, the character, movement, accent, breath, and most intimate feeling [of a passage]: in short,

everything that cannot be said with words, everything that
constitutes music's *ineffable* aspects—music's very essence.[53]

Almost at the beginning, "In manus tuas" contains the standard
fifths in the horns (the so-called *quinte dei corni*, or horn fifths, in
this case doubled by the oboes), and had to be—as the maestro
said during rehearsal—music "that comes from afar." With that
he aimed immediately to point out bars 8–12 (and, by extension,
bars 88–92 in the reprise):

The evening of the concert, that passage was incredibly allur-
ing, because it effectively rejected generic melancholy and, to
my eyes, became tenderly allusive. The following day I opened
the score, where I found confirmation of everything that Muti,
with the expertise of a dramaturge, had achieved that previous
evening. Indeed, the horns are not missing throughout Haydn's
music for *The Seven Last Words of Christ*. They are actually a part
of the ensemble from the very beginning. But there is not a single moment—with the exception of the fragment in bars 50–52
of the finale, "Terremoto," which drowns in a fortissimo—in
which the couple plays according to the typical overblown sixth-
fifth-third formula. That is, by nature, the instrument's formula,
so much so that it justifies the popular term *horn fifths* (even the
colossal *Emperor* Concerto relies on it from beginning to end).

In *The Seven Last Words*, however, the opposite happens. The horns almost always play a series of octaves or the succession octave-fifth. Haydn carefully "saved" the formula for the final number, redeeming it and elevating it to fulfill the role of a noble metaphor, deploying it to express "In manus tuas, Domine, commendo animam meam" (Into thy hands, O Lord, I commend my soul) when Jesus goes home after the suffering of the Passion. (Even today during the leave-taking rite, expressions of this sort are used: "he returns today to the house of the father.") It is a highly nostalgic passage, a memory of the homeland that in many of Schubert's *Lieder* provides the illusion of a return for the wayfarer, or expresses the deep pain of someone with no home or country, the *heimatlos*. This is a particularly German tradition. Even popular collections for home use are rife with such passages, and there is no fear of repeating the concept too much (it is irrelevant that, in people's homes, the piece is likely to end up played on the piano rather than by two horns: everyone gladly accepts such an "accommodation"!). Although there are many more such examples, Haydn's *melos* at that point is quite basic, and it is identical to the one we hear when Gretel whispers, "Ein Männlein steht im Walde ganz still und stumm" at the edge of the forest in Engelbert Humperdinck's opera *Hänsel und Gretel:*

Im Walde.

Sehr ruhig (♩=66)
GRETEL   *(leise vor sich hin summend)*

Ein Männ-lein steht im Wal - de ganz still und   stumm,

Therefore, compared to the later incarnation with its added flourish, the early version from 1785 (the year *The Seven Last Words of Christ* was composed) contains a few hints—if you will pardon the didactic chronology—of pre-Romantic flavor. In an opera composed completely of *Empfindungen*, impressions, and almost entirely devoid of any hint of *Malerei*, or "painterly" signs (I count just three: aside from the "Terremoto," there is the "cadence" in "Consummatum," the "rain" in "Sitio," and the "homeland" in "In manus"), Muti impeccably captured the mimetic aspect. It is reinforced by the echo effect—often discounted but providing a theatrical touch—offered by the final measures played by the flutes and horns. For orchestra musicians, he translated the indication *sempre più piano* with the words "as if the light were no more." In the echo, that subphrase is repeated *pp*, and there, too, the maestro intuited the sporadic nature of "sonorous painting" and—I cannot help repeating myself—brought it *to the stage* with great precision.

In 1994, he replicated that atmosphere with the exact same instinctive, unconscious, (I dare say) sureness at the Teatro Alighieri di Ravenna,[54] where he was conducting *Norma*. In the extreme passage of the lovers' dramatic confrontation, a motif of sixteenth notes reminiscent of the shivers played in the symphony is followed by an in-unison fragment of an ascending scale—a solution taken for granted following the fermata at the dominant chord—introduces the duet "In mia mano alfin tu sei" and is preceded by the distinctive passage played by the horns:

I had always found those subphrases not only too predictable, but also overly mimetic, colorful, allusive—in short, too much all around, and therefore jarring in a finale of such austere tragedy as that of *Norma*. Yet that evening the horns were truly very distant, almost imperceptible, and hinted at an echo effect that conjured up a feeling of nostalgia and memory (such feelings, obviously, are destined to repeat themselves). For the first time I understood the beauty of a "place" I thought I knew inside out, and Muti had led me to that place, where as Guillaume Apollinaire so sweetly put it, "Les souvenirs sont cors de chasse / Dont meurt le bruit parmi le vent" (Memories are hunting horns / Whose sound dies out along the wind).[55]

Such unwitting "creativity" is what the audience asks of every artist worthy of that title. One day, just a few hours before a performance of Verdi's *Requiem* in the Basilica di San Lorenzo in Florence, Muti gave the Orchestra Giovanile Italiana some words of warning that proved he is a true artist—someone who hates "the phantasm of anything packaged, canned."[56] Muti said, "Don't always just think *like that*! Watch me tonight and follow me: there'll be something different—I still don't know what I'll do *tonight*!" (And when he realized basso Stefan Elenkov

understood not a single word of the Latin text and therefore ran
the risk of tripping over each passage, he said, "Tonight, whatever happens, just look at me!") In his essay "Il monologo" (The
Monologue) Carmelo Bene uses an example of an orchestra
conductor to scold an actor who minimizes his role onstage by
turning into a mere narrator, an "epic-demonstrative-caption"
of the text:

> An orchestra conductor who, after the last "dress rehearsal,"
> abandons his baton during the "premiere" and is then com-
> pletely capable of recriminating "that things didn't go as they
> should have, beginning with the interpreters, musicians, and
> singers" who'd have done better to risk everything; at least
> then, maybe, something involuntary, irresponsible, *gratuitous*
> could pop up from that huge window with red velvet curtains
> opened onto the indifferent consensus of the audience which,
> by now *drugged* by the *dead* text, has gathered there to ask for
> another dose of tranquilizer.[57]

It goes without saying that precisely because of these characteristics, one should not listen to recordings of a conductor like
Riccardo Muti. Sitting in front of speakers and anesthetizing
oneself with the same effect thirty times over is wrong, as with
repetition that effect becomes a dead, "ill effect"!

Maybe it was just that kind of steadiness that disappointed
him one afternoon at the Villa la Torraccia in Fiesole, when he
instructed the musicians, "Let's leave order to everyone else!"
This satisfied my patriotic pride, which for a moment took an
anti-Philarmoniker turn. That instruction pulled us out of the

"international style" common to the recording industry, giving players the possibility of creating a "national" sound and saving them from the precipitous present-day trend of reification. Rehearsing Paisiello and warning the musicians of the imminent *fp*:

in Milan, he assured them that it was a trifle—they just needed to stop their bows immediately and put "weight on the left of the bow with that *p*, otherwise the sound will die"—while "in Vienna it always takes ten minutes to explain that to the orchestra, if you don't want them to play the usual *f* followed by the usual diminuendo!"[58] This must be a fairly common error in German-speaking countries. As early as the end of the nineteenth century, critics remarked, "Strings and winds have the habit of playing a forte-diminuendo instead of the prescribed *fp*. This blunder is committed by almost all orchestras, and destroys much of the effect the composer aimed to achieve. In order to allow the note to go immediately from the initial forte to the following piano, you have to ask the strings to hold the bow back a bit after the attack, and the winds to hold back their breath."[59]

Furthermore, the resolute, dynamic opposition so important onstage is also a metaphor for drama—that is, the genre whose basic, "primary character remains the representation of conflict";[60] Muti emphasizes that model at the beginning of the finale of the first act of *Nina*, when the quartet attacks with a brief, forte *coulé* (a rising passage of sixteenth and thirty-second notes), followed by eighth notes played staccato and piano. For him, in spite of the passage's sustained tempo and legato, the bar division needs to serve as a real boundary:

"They are two *different* things: the first is a push; the second is a simple stroll." (That same finale would then be ended with a Più allegro to be played "a bit crazily . . ." and then he forms a circle on each hand with his thumb and index finger in the universal symbol for *okay*, as if to say, "too perfect.")

During the performance of *Don Giovanni* in Ravenna, none of us knew anything about *those* recitatives—a detail that unexpectedly conditioned the entire performance. Not only did they fulfill Mozart's desire (in a letter sent to his father from Mannheim on November 12, 1778, he enthusiastically wrote that "in [Georg] Benda's piece they speak over the music and during the music: almost all recitatives in opera would best be treated that way"), but they also provided real surprises throughout the three-hour performance. The form of the accompaniment—at the maestro's behest, though it seemed bizarre at first, with a note, a chord, and many, many silences—enchanted the audience from the very first number. It also gave the storyline a euphoric quickness that the usual chords, played one after the other, and the intolerable cadences of the harpsichord tend to deaden. One major critic—who would have preferred, legitimately, a "more complete, more balanced" conductor—deemed all of this (apparently too new and *à la Mozart!*) "overly ambitious." He was handing us the plot, and with the plot the entire drama. At the end of the first act, I treasured the famous three little orchestras playing three different dances, a passage often noted in critical commentary but hard to hear in the theater because "law and order" conductors tend to blur the edges and let them blend together while one of the three takes the lead (often, by default, the minuet). Never before had I heard the ensembles clash so distressingly, and I was finally able to appreciate fully the passage's harsh, grating sound—giving it the flavor of *truth*. The entire physical stage space was in the maestro's hands, and he brought it to life as only the best *metteurs en scène* can.

On the same subject, consider just one more first-act finale, from Rossini's *La donna del lago*. I wonder if anyone before Muti had understood that the onstage band is not really just a band (if not in Hans Werner Henze's heroic sense), but rather the orchestra's generous double, which deserves to be returned to its true splendor:

Is this yet another problem solved 170 years after the work's "premiere"? I believe so, and it was resolved so well that, I must confess, when I heard it I began to wonder why Muti had not had the courage to do the same thing that Wagner and Mahler had dared to do before: write an *ex novo* instrumentation for the offstage orchestra. Yet I was nevertheless extremely grateful that he even brought that question spontaneously to mind.

Once again, it was entirely the maestro's doing that the space was completely "filled" (à la Rossini) and that he had chosen (à la Artaud) a singularly "concrete language" with which to make it speak. I therefore realize that the analogy I drew earlier between Muti and the *metteur en scène* was something of a free association—one of those reactions where the heart overpowers the wits. That is precisely why listening to Paisiello's *Nina* calls to mind Artaud's wonderful essay "Metaphysics and the Mise en Scène," which says that theater is created with the lightning strikes—"coup de foudre" *id est* "coup de théâtre"!—that illuminate Lot's daughters in the eponymous painting by Lucas van Leyden: "Its emotion . . . is visible even from a distance; it affects the mind with an almost thunderous visual harmony, intensely active throughout the painting, yet to be gathered from a single glance."[61] A near translation of these lines can be read in a passage where Carmelo Bene clarifies his own idea of theater: "Like fireworks at night, words piercingly illuminate the sky, each pulsating with its own incandescent life, forming phrases; their sense

is soon lost and already other fireworks shine brilliantly, way
up there, beyond meaning."[62] Such were all the subphrases and
motifs in *Nina*. The final number ("Oh che dolce sospirare!"),
played after the maestro had jokingly instructed the musicians,
"fasten your seatbelts," saw the very slow choral "insertions"
isolated from "Figlio è amor della pietà" become sound as rhetorical contrast in a whirlwind that verged on wildness:

These stood apart from the rest of the number with the prestige
of a *noema*, a brief homophonic section that bursts in at the end
of the ancient polyphonic motet,[63] and then, with the prowess of
the final acceleration, tumbles down onto the cadenced chords.
As the maestro instructed that the musicians *stringere* more than
they had dreamed possible, he said, "These are formulas! C'mon,
let's go!! It isn't Beethoven!!!"[64] It was similar to the end of *Don
Giovanni*, the part that struck Mahler as an embarrassment, a
useless obstacle before the hero's death: the survivors swoop
in from stage right ("Ah dov'è il perfido?") and the spotlights

follow them, yet it is not the director but rather Muti—you can see it—who creates a different, *other* light with sound alone. He pushes the Allegro assai to the edge, then halts for the lovers' scene ("Or che tutti o mio tesoro"). In the darkened theater, the audience understands that he has invented a "scene" completely different from no. 15. Everything is fine. It is perfect just *like this*.

These are Shakespearian moments of "perfect illusion" (to quote Stendhal) and the instances of sound and fury that T. S. Eliot wrote of having endured in the work of Seneca and Shakespeare. Eliot and Stendhal, two who really understood theater! In those very instants the process of identification steals the viewer from himself and transforms a simple "experience" into "something really lived," no longer an *Erfahrung* but rather *Erlebnis*. The maestro's style distinguishes among moments of heightened expression and courageously isolates them as he knows best—without the work as a whole suffering, and without losing the "unifying coherence" of music that Amadeus Hoffmann (not to mention Aristotle!) established. In the 102 measures of the incredibly long "Confitebor" of the *Vesperae*, for example, bars 63–65 were for him "the *only* moment of great poetry in the entire piece":

Muti's performance of *Manon Lescaut* was remarkable because of the incomparable reminiscence of the minuet twenty measures from the end. Normally, this is just barely "heard," and many conductors impudently leave it out completely. That evening, however, it seemed to be drowning, mysterious and unrecognizable, and so an audience member would try to hang on to it with the same desperation as the protagonist. Like the mother's eyes that in Andersen's tale saw in the well of Death's garden "the other life, which held only sorrow, poverty, fear, and woe,"[65]or like Roy Lichtenstein's comic-strip girl crying, "I don't care! I'd rather sink than call Brad for help!" it appeared at the bottom of a lake.

On the evening of December 10, 1970, the impatient clang of the tin drum burst onto the scene just as a disheartened baritone recited his heart's suffering (the most basic and unbearable: unrequited love) and the music aimed to beguile them with an "affection" as clumsy as love of country. Suddenly, an extraordinarily powerful fanfare "filled up the place"—as Rossini would have put it.[66] It had the same weight as any other set decoration, an unknown prop, as worn and useless as the junk hawked by a pawn shop. That evening, a youthful thirty-year-old Riccardo Muti debuted with *I puritani*. "Je dis que la scène est un lieu physique et concret qui demande qu'on le remplisse, et qu'on lui fasse parler son langage concret":[67] the drums that sounded from all sides, *Verso Prometeo* (Toward *Prometeo*) in an ultramodern take on the *Quadrivium* or *Répons,* were found to be different, and so crisply visible that they miraculously made the presence of the director seem almost unnecessary:[68]

The next day I wondered what the actors had been doing in the meantime, where the chorus was, and whether with the whole thing had been given a backdrop, some sort of overlay to indicate the season, along with all the other period details provided in the libretto that seemed to come straight out of a historical novel. I forgot all about Sandro Sequi; indeed, I no longer remembered anything. That was when I realized that for me the director—and "theater," in the worst sense of the word—had been replaced by that dark-haired kid in the middle of the orchestra to whom I had been shouting "Bravo" almost all evening. I shouted it especially loudly after Elvira's arias, because there was no doubt as to who had hit a home run! Not because of the gregarious spirit so odious to the Canetti of *Masse und Macht*,[69] the Adorno of "Meisterschaft,"[70] and the Hindemith of

Interpreten,[71] nor because of a certain exuberance that needed to be snuffed out, but rather because of something infinitely simpler: a feeling of genuine identification. Since Aristotle's time, the theatergoer has been someone in search of an instantaneous, quick, unexpected view of everything that is different, of everything beyond the everyday world, and of a life—of the baritone, in this case—that has touched us one day without our even realizing it. The next morning, in his review, Pinzauti conceded at the start, "The allure of lyric theater lies also in a 'bravo' yelled at the least opportune moment: ultimately, it is a sign of life and participation,"[72] and I felt like a mischievous boy, as content as De André's titular *bombarolo,* or bomber.[73]

These may seem like highly personal reactions, a whim or a meaningless record of a type of nostalgia that I ought to keep to myself, coming as it does largely from the subconscious. But perhaps it is a sign of something more than that, and perhaps it can be used to describe the nature of the person and the phenomenon in sturdier terms. Carmelo Bene's written warnings suggest as much: woe to the director's work if it simply reproduces the text with the timid respect of someone content to read without heeding the desire for everything to be rendered as if new in the penumbra of the theater, and woe to those who dare to ruin melodrama, when the music itself is already a kind of written instruction and the score an impeccable substitute for the script, as it illuminates situations and the plot with tools much more explosive than any word.

In the minds of most audience members, the theatrical tradition of the Italian school began with Toscanini. Over the years, its genealogy has grown like some epic "family tree" to include De

Sabata, Gui, Gavazzeni, and the sublime Carlo Maria Giulini (I say this literally, meaning the kind of sublime "that, transcending the confines of mere beauty, elevates our soul from low, earthly things and lifts it into the realm of the infinite").[74] Naturally this lineage also includes conductors like Votto and Serafin, the keepers of opera's secrets, invisibly at work in the darkness of the orchestral "pit." Like Verdi and Puccini before them, they have all passed on the legacy, and at the end of the sixties, along came Muti. In accordance with Italian musical custom, he conducts both the symphonic repertoire and melodrama—without making hierarchical distinctions between the two, as the former is enlivened by the "representative" strength and scenic power of the latter, and the latter is treated with the dignity and scrupulousness normally granted the former. The *vexata quaestio* of "expression" is resolved in an instant: for Muti, music—whether accompanied by a libretto or not—must always "speak"; it must always communicate something to an audience, in the quickest, most genuine terms possible, respecting the text—it goes without saying—but reproducing it with a *creative* (innate? instinctive? intuitive?) impetus that matches that of its author (hence my earlier reference to Adorno's paradoxical "transcription").

Melodrama offers an extraordinary opportunity for interaction with the audience, because each note carries meaning that goes beyond mere plot. The new plot, the primarily musical one, is necessary and uninterrupted, and it found in Muti the "director" prophesied in Carmelo Bene's *La voce di Narciso*—a director capable of drawing out the meaning of even its most obscure content. Believe it or not, it was as if the role of the director became superfluous: it became *his* role in a kind of peculiar and theretofore unheard of *Regietheater* or "directional theater." His visionary instinct allowed him to translate an emotional "situation" in the lines of a musical phrase or song with a liveliness that was solidly convincing. This provided the highest level of experience possible at the theater, which for centuries (forgive me for repeating myself) has consisted of a few great things: identification, pity, pathos, and fear.

I came to understand this on that long-ago December 1, and I felt it again to an unsurpassable degree on an afternoon in June 1996, when I happened to be at the Comunale di Bologna to see Muti conduct the last orchestra rehearsals of *Cavalleria rusticana* before it was to be performed in Ravenna for ten days straight, with neither singers nor chorus and—obviously—no stage set. I felt I had enjoyed Mascagni as much as anyone possibly could. And the absence of the libretto, evidently mitigated by the short plot summary I still remembered, was no obstacle to understanding—rather, it allowed me to have a reaction unlike any I had ever had at more traditional performances.

Just to be clear, something similar happens to me if I listen to the famous recording of Toscanini rehearsing, with only an orchestra, the second part of the second act of Verdi's *La Traviata*—the gathering at Flora's house. To give credit where credit is due, I really do not need to see onstage activity, because the conductor does it all. He is a surrogate for the director; he replaces the libretto and explains, through the imprecise means of musical notes alone, how true Artaud's vision of theater—in his "metaphysical" essay he compares it to the towering mass of a pyramid—really is. What did the Egyptians build in the desert if not a scenic mountain that grows out of nothing (with "nothing" understood to be the Pharaoh's small corpse—that is, the text)? "To abstain from making use of the stage," Artaud writes, is "like someone who, with the pyramids for burying the corpse of a pharaoh, used the pretext that the pharaoh's corpse occupied only a niche, and had the pyramids blown up. He would have blown up at the same time the whole magical and philosophical system for which the niche was only the point of departure and the corpse the condition."[75]

Maybe I can better explain the feeling I had by once again quoting a fellow Italian—specifically, Carmelo Bene—on childhood memories:

> Basically, for me, the only theater was the "lyric" kind: sounds, lights, splendors, extravagances, a spectacle where no one spoke the way people do in everyday life. To my young ears, those "prose" people seemed so natural—twice or thrice I went to see such a show—that it sounded as if they were just mumbling and grumbling at one another.. . .
> "When do they sing?" I pestered my grandmother.
> "You silly, these actors don't sing, they talk."
> "They just talk, and they're paid to do that?"
> "Of course, why not, you want them to talk for free?"
> "But this theater is the same one we go to to hear music and singing."
> "Sheesh! These actors have nothing to do with music. They don't have the right voices."
> "Well then, what did we come for?"[76]

This autobiographical episode is striking because it conveys the great actor's deep-rooted passion for melodrama and opera. In operatic theater people sing, while in ordinary theater they do not. Thus his childhood memory becomes a sort of apologue, attesting not only to his genuine fervor for the genre, but also to what Bene thought of theater. As everyone knows, he saw it the same way Artaud did: "A formal aphasia regularly occurs during costume changes, in points of negligence, in certain awkward costume combinations, off-pitch notes, etc. In such incidents, stuttering, inhuman spasms, grunts, convulsive coughing fits, cold and hot sweats, and senseless calling out dominate the stage set."[77] He continues: "The a priori dramaturge is conceivable only if his script—steering clear of the overly discomforting, habitual back-and-forth volley of prose 'jokes'—is instead already the plan for a real spectacle; if, much as with the specific nature of music, it is a score that will be reinvented by the execution on the night of its celebration."[78]

During the costume changes, God willing, not a single word or verse of the tragic text is to be reproduced, thereby achieving the ideal that marked Bene's childhood experience: the actors cease telling each other what is happening onstage. A contrast between the text and the temporarily mute actor sets language to one side and to the other everything else foreign to language, as the actor is degraded to a state of "aphasia." This is the adult theory about his childhood experience with his grandmother. "Such incidents" end up "dominating." From a scenic point of view, everything on the other side of the balance outweighs the linguistic side.

A preference for "stuttering," and in particular "senseless calling out," pushing language to one side and everything else to the other—as something residual, not clearly identified, and vast—is not an isolated paradox. Rather, it is one side in a debate that has raged for over two millennia and runs through more or less the entire history of theater. It goes against Aristotle, who—with his passion for the "text" over any and all accessory or show-related elements—stands at the opposite end. That said, becoming a melodrama fan is imperative. Bene takes issue with "dialogue" slapped together from volleyed jokes and contrasts "prose" theater with its festive staging (the two terms used in Aristotle's *Poetics* are *lexis* and *opsis*). In other words, there is wretched theater on the one hand and real theater on the other. That is why, in an attempt to share his own poetics with the public, he latches on to opera. He develops an affection for the *score* because it establishes the convincing, essential analogy between theater and melodrama, where, substituting the score for the script, the "dramaturge" director finally disappears, making way for the composer and, of course, the orchestra conductor.

This kind of paradigm helps me to explain the disposition, virtues, and nature of Riccardo Muti as an orchestra conductor. In keeping with Bene's perspective (whereby the text is theater's enemy, and theater deserves something else), the staging reveals that the orchestra's "accompaniment" is a precious addition—and it is therefore neither the time nor place for chit-chat, "Socratism," or pure "language." That is what caused my sentimental incident at the performance of *Cavalleria rusticana* as a symphonic poem in Bologna. It is also behind my sudden curiosity—going back to December 1970!—about the ultra-marked accents the maestro put on the *ménage à trois* in the climax at the end of the first act of *I Puritani*: "Ah! che festi?" / "La prigioniera!" / "Dessa io son!" / "Vien ... tua voce altera or col ferro sosterrai." / "No, con lei tu illeso andrai" ("Ah? What have you done?" / "The prisoner!" / "Truly I am she." / "Come, maintain now thy lofty language with thy sword." / "No, thou shalt go with her in safety."):

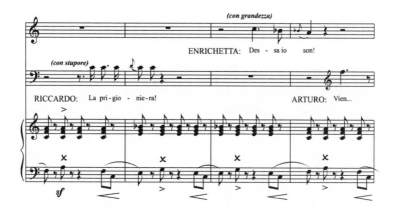

Muti ably translates Verdi's "not so long from now, you will only be able to see my music"[79] and Artaud's "the ear . . . is as moved by it as the eye"[80] for the orchestra musicians with "the scenic word": "Like making a face!" I, personally, also see this in certain unforgettable passages of *Nabucco*, *Nina*, and *The Marriage of Figaro*:[81]

In short, in the years of *Regietheater*, melodrama was the absolute paradigm of theater in its noblest sense:

> The presence of a director is even more grotesque and intolerable in lyric opera.. . . . [He] usually makes the situation worse with the "morbidity" of the set and furnishings: I cannot listen to Mozart without the visual punishment of having to look at a sitting room that is "just so." The lights, forever ignoring the music, serve only to "see" and set the color (when the weather is good) of daybreaks and nightfalls already lit or dimmed by the score. Verdi was prophetic: "not so long from now, you will only be able to see my music.". . . In Verdi music is always action, and also has a lot of "calibrated" effects, extremely calculated, that cannot support the vulgarity of being doubled visually as well.. . . In the great oblivion of golden-age (and gold-staged) theater, the word was music, until the advent of the Euripidean-Socratic *epos* ruined tragic poetry with its dialectics. This war senselessly declared on the moral motives of intoxication necessitated a gossipy, long-winded prologue, defrauding theater of its "metaphysical consolation."[82]

These lines, from Bene's aforementioned "Il monologo"—perhaps his most important writing—stand before us with the simplicity of a manual: on the one hand, the music of melodrama is so theatrical you can almost *see* it more than you hear it, which is precisely why anything the director might do is destined to become redundant; on the other, the text and its dialectical miseries irreparably spoil the spectator's inebriated experience. The irresistible construction of the notes is also a regal metaphor for theater and the mise-en-scène.

To sum up: Aristotle, reading the tragedians, attended to the written word and paid little attention to the represented text (in its two aspects, *conspectus* and *apparatus*).[83] Many—among the moderns, Artaud especially—reversed that hierarchy, and Carmelo Bene, as intent as Artaud on removing from theater everything that, when staged, drowned out the text, discovered melodrama was the ideal genre for representing the text, because the libretto (text) steps aside and is nothing when compared to the music (Theater) that amplifies it. The detested script is replaced by the score, and the composer takes the place of the abhorred director.

On the one hand, we cannot even perceive the composer without the orchestra conductor acting as a magical go-between; on the other, not everyone has as keen a sense of the stage as Riccardo Muti. And therein lies his art.

As Nietzsche wrote in the spring of 1880:

The poet brings our instinctive desire to know into *play*, the composer, on the contrary, lets it *rest*; will the poet and the composer ever be able to get along? When we abandon ourselves completely to music, we have no words in mind, and that is a great relief. As soon as we listen to words again and try to reach some conclusion—in short, when we understand the text—our reaction to the music immediately becomes super-

ficial, we tie it to concepts, we compare it to feelings, we look
for symbolic results. All of this is quite entertaining, but the
deep and singular magic that gave our thought some rest, that
blessed twilight that has for once dimmed the bright daylight
of the spirit, all of that disappears. When, on the other hand,
you no longer understand the words, everything returns to
order: this, happily, is the rule. One should always prefer the
worst texts, because they do not attract the attention, but rather
almost ask to be overlooked.[84]

In other words, he felt more or less the same way Muti does: "It
doesn't matter if you don't understand it at all, because what mat-
ters is what it says to you personally, the emotions it makes you
feel—don't worry in the least about what the know-it-alls think."[85]

Notes

CHAPTER ONE

1   Italian historian and antifascist activist.—Trans.

2   Horace, *Epistles*, I: 2.38–39: *Quæ lædunt oculum festinas demere;
    si quid est animum, differs curandi tempus in annum* (If anything
    affects your eye, you hasten to have it removed; but if anything
    affects [eats] your mind, you postpone the term of cure for a
    year).

3   From the entry dated Wednesday, October 26, "Un tratto gener-
    oso" ("A Generous Deed"): Franti apes Crossi's mother; Crossi
    throws an inkwell at Franti, but he dodges and it hits the teacher;
    Garrone, an innocent witness, takes the blame to clear the rest of
    the class. Published in English as *Heart*, trans. Isabel F. Hapgood
    (New York: Crowell, 1887).

4   Italian actor, director, and singer-songwriter.—Trans.

5   This near play on words reflects a coincidence: the doctor's last
    name, Muti, sounds related to the term *mutuati*, patients of the
    Mutua, or National Health Service.—Trans.

6   Renato Fucini, *Le veglie di Neri* (Florence: G. Barbèra, 1883).
    This passage is titled "Dolci ricordi" (Sweet Memories), in
    which Fucini confesses to his father that he's lost some money
    gambling.

7   "C'mon, Luigi, move it!" in dialect.

8   "Power is a ruse, glory fades, and time flies."

9   The Roman goddess of death, corpses, and funerals.—Trans.

10 Ernesto De Martino, *Morte e pianto rituale: Dal lamento funebre antico al pianto di Maria* (1958; Turin: Bollati Boringhieri, 1977).

11 Ibid., chapter 2, "Il lamento funebre lucano," 97. De Martino writes: "In general, funerary laments in present-day Lucania are performed by the deceased's relatives, without contributions from hired or professional mourners. Nevertheless, the public memory of such 'prefiche,' the women called upon to add their song at funeral ceremonies, lives on, and refers to a relatively recent past. The once-famous mourners of Senise were called upon in nearby towns to lend their prized voices, as were those of Pisticci and a few other villages. Currently, professional mourning is viewed with some degree of shame and embarrassment, and one village often accuses the next of this practice, without such accusations holding much truth or ever being proven" (79).

12 Dante Alighieri, *Inferno*, XXIII: 3.

13 "I'd like to sing / the holy joy, / of God's beauty, / of great dignity. / He is embodied in the pious Virgin / leaving Mary her virginity / with such love, with such love: / as the Holy Spirit would have it."—Trans.

14 "Povera Rosa" is perhaps the most popular of the funeral marches local bands would play at various "stations" along town roads during the main procession on Good Friday. Its title likely comes from the moving epicede "Povera Rosa!" by Salvatore Di Giacomo, in *Poesie e prose* (Milan: Mondadori, 1977), 242.

15 Vincenzo Vitale, *Il pianoforte a Napoli nell'Ottocento* (Naples: Bibliopolis, 1983).

16 In the Italian school system, the "classical lyceum" is a secondary school distinguished from other curricula by its focus on Latin and Greek language and literature, as well as the humanities as a whole.—Trans.

CHAPTER TWO

1   State (public) high school.—Trans.

2   "Maestro, cumme state? I' ve tengo ogne ghiuorno 'nnanze a
     ll'uocchie!"

3   Light modifications in notes' duration made to a piece for the
     sake of greater expression.

CHAPTER THREE

1   In Camillo Mastrocinque's 1956 film, Antonio and Peppino
     Caponi (Totò and Peppino De Filippo) go to Milan to visit their
     nephew Gianni (Teddy Reno), who has fallen hopelessly in love
     with a ballerina named Marisa (Dorian Gray) and followed her
     north.

2   This is a verse of the poem "Caporetto 1917: Sonada quasi
     ona fantasia" (1919) by the great poet Delio Tessa, who wrote
     primarily in dialect. In *L'è el dì di mort, alegher! De là del mur*
     (Turin: Einaudi, 1999), 55.

3   Dino Risi's 1962 film tells the story of a road trip that comes
     to a tragic end: Bruno (Vittorio Gassman) adores his car, a
     Lancia Aurelia B 24. He and Roberto (Jean-Louis Trintignant)
     give a ride to a farmer who questions its horsepower, so Bruno
     launches into a reckless race, advising him to hold on to his hat:
     "Nonne', sta attento che te vola er Borsalino!"

4   "Borsalineide," in *Ti à piaciato?!!* (Sesto San Giovanni: Madella,
     1915), 91–95. "You must remember / we're leaving tomorrow
     morning: / it would be sad to go / without your Borsalino."

5   Counterpoint was developed in Flanders in the fourteenth century.

6   "Guè, Ricca', ch' ee fatto? mme pare Barièllo."

7   "U cazzo co' cappiello."

8   Radio Audizioni Italiane was renamed Radiotelevisione Itali-
     ana in 1954, but the broadcasting entity, along with its excellent
     orchestra, continued to use the initials RAI.—Trans.

9   In the aforementioned film *Totò, Peppino e la malafemmina,*
    where the two southern visitors are always bundled up to protect
    themselves from what they perceive to be the terrifying cold of
    Milan.—Trans.

10 From the Italian *verismo* movement in literature and music,
    whose champions in opera included Pietro Mascagni, Ruggero
    Leoncavallo, and Giacomo Puccini.—Trans.

11 At bar 333ff. of the last movement.

CHAPTER FOUR

1   The main ensemble of the Maggio Musicale Fiorentino, an an-
    nual springtime music festival held in Florence.—Trans.

2   Leonardo Pinzauti, "Richter e Muti: successo a sorpresa," *La
    Nazione,* June 20, 1968. This was the first of Pinzauti's many re-
    views of Muti, all collected in *Riccardo Muti al Teatro Comunale
    di Firenze, 1968–1982* (Pisa: ETS, 2009).

3   Pinzauti, "Vivo successo del direttore napoletano e del clarinet-
    tista Detalmo Corneti," *La Nazione,* October 29, 1968.

4   See *Atti del primo congresso internazionale di musica* (Florence,
    April 30–May 4, 1933) (Florence: Le Monnier, 1935).

5   Vittorio Gui, *Battute d'aspetto: Meditazioni di un musicista
    militante* (Florence: Monsalvato, 1944), 110. An early version
    of this article had appeared in the *Corriere d'Italia* in 1914. It's
    worth noting that the other famous apologia for Brahms, Arnold
    Schönberg's *Brahms the Progressive,* dates to 1933, and the paral-
    lel date supports the case for Gui's importance.

6   Gui, *Battute d'aspetto,* 6.

7   Pinzauti refers to this, with a touch of Wagnerian/Toscanin-
    ian disapproval, in his article "Entusiasmo di altri tempi per *I
    puritani* al Comunale," first published in *La Nazione,* December
    2, 1970.

8   Those who aim to perform so-called early music "philologically," or formalistically, needn't think that literalism obliges the use of a limited number of musicians. It's obvious that orchestras were smaller in Mozart's and Bach's day than they are now, but in light of certain clues we must admit that even they were gladdened by the few occasions when they were able to enlarge the ensemble.

9   ". . . di farci parer l'opera più breve del solito." Fedele D'Amico, "La bandiera rossa ha ingannato i critici," in *Tutte le cronache musicali* (Rome: Bulzoni, 2000), 749.

10   *Ursus in the Valley of the Lions*, a 1961 fantasy adventure directed by Carlo Ludovico Bragaglia.—Trans.

11   "Go ahead and open the curtains: one sole spectator with the wits of Plato is worth more than a full house." This phrase concludes Gluck's famous preface to *Paride ed Elena*: "I do not hope that my *Paride* might be a greater success than *Alceste*. Regarding the intent to have the desired effect of influencing [other] musical composers, alas, I foresee ever-greater obstacles. Yet despite that I shall not cease my attempts to achieve good [musical] design, and should I obtain the support of Your Highness I shall gladly repeat: *Tolle siparium, sufficit mihi unus Plato pro cuncto populo*" (Vienna: Trattner, 1770), x, cited in *Christoph Willibald Gluck: Sämtliche Werke*, ser. 1, vol. 4, ed. Rudolf Gerber (Kassel: Bärenreiter, 1954), xiii. It was extremely popular and, to give just one example, Francesco Albergati—perhaps in response to a letter in which Giuseppe Baretti accused him of too easily finding success—used it in the preface to the 1787 edition of his complete theatrical works; see Ernesto Masi, *La vita, i tempi, gli amici di Francesco Albergati commediografo del secolo XVIII* (Bologna: Zanichelli, 1878), 269.

12   Roman Vlad, *Strawinsky* (Turin: Einaudi, 1958).

13   A town near Florence.—Trans.

14   Gianotto Bastianelli, *Pietro Mascagni* (Naples: Ricciardi, 1910).

15 "L'ha detto i' Muti!"

16 "Battle on the Piave River," a patriotic song by Giovanni Gaeta
(writing under the pseudonym E. A. Mario) following the events
of June 1918. The speaker made a pun with the conductor's last
name (with *muti* also meaning "mute"): "The footsoldiers were
mute that night, / they had to be silent and go forward."—
Trans.

17 D'Amico, "Spontini gioca con l'algebra," in *Tutte le cronache*,
1045ff.

18 "The result—thanks in part to the pregnant dialectic between
the intimate phrasing of his voice and the visual impact of his
figure—is a *Macbeth* who's more suffocated than he is violent.
[His] dignity has been devastated by guilt yet is nevertheless
recognizable, and ultimately oppressed by a compassionate and
piteous sadness." D'Amico, "Macbeth a bassa voce," in *Tutte le
cronache*, 1173.

19 In act I, scene 2, Lady Macbeth reads the letter aloud: "I
met them on the day of victory, and was stunned by what I
heard."—Trans.

20 D'Amico, "Quel regista è un infedele," in *Tutte le cronache*, 1695.

CHAPTER FIVE

1   Paid mourners; see Chapter 1.—Trans.

2   "Bravo Muti, che fa il *Così fan tutte* e *Così* va al massacro," a
wordplay on *così*, "thus."—Trans.

3   The German term, literally "entertainment music," is roughly
translatable as "easy listening" or "light music." Of course,
the elevated tenor of the German and Austrian musical traditions grants such a term relatively high respect, and also tends
to hold commercial musical productions in higher esteem than
other cultures do—consider the work of Kurt Weill and Norbert
Schultze, to name only two.

4   As readers will have noted, this is a nod to Verdi's opera *La forza del destino*, the "force of destiny."

CHAPTER SIX

1   In Italy, a *notaio* is somewhere between a notary public and a lawyer, and the profession is highly regarded.

2   Gui, *Battute d'aspetto*, 129ff.

CHAPTER SEVEN

1   Benedetto Craxi was Italian Socialist Party chairman (1976–93) and prime minister (1983–87).—Trans.

2   Cuts made under the austerity budget passed in late 2010 led to the temporary closing of many theaters and opera houses as musicians, singers, and others protested an almost 40 percent drop in government subsidies.—Trans.

3   "Tutti nani nell'*Ernani*!" and "Eccomi qua, m'hanno ridotto 'er nano'!" Both exclamations include wordplay on *nani*, "dwarves," that is lost in English; *er* is Roman dialect for *il*.—Trans.

4   The hundredth anniversary of Verdi's death.

5   "Not the ink, but the sense," from Saint Paul's famous passage urging readers not to pharisaically keep strictly to the "letter" of a written text: "For as much as you are manifestly declared to be the letter of Christ ministered by us, written not with ink, but with the Spirit . . . not in tablets of stone, but in fleshy tablets of the heart" (2 Cor. 3:3): it isn't the ink that counts, but rather the sense, and even one's common sense in interpreting it.

6   Giuseppe Piermarini, architect of La Scala (1776–78).—Trans.

7   Singers' substitution of one note for another in order to better display their abilities.

8   The original Italian refers to the Breccia di Porta Pia, the historic breaching of the city walls during the Italian army's capture

of Rome on September 20, 1870. The author draws a parallel between that watershed event and this significant performance, which began to break down a long-standing barrier in the history of La Scala and the broader operatic tradition.—Trans.

9   This passage was written in dialect: "Oi ma'! Siente, . . . sa' che m'aggio sunnato? D'aveie fatto nu straviso a chillo llà! Puozz'ess'acciso! O steve pa' accirere a chillo llà!"—Trans.

10 A sixteenth-century Italian mercenary leader and nobleman, widely considered a national hero.—Trans.

11 This line is contentious: ᵹerbino is literally "doormat," whereas the related term ᵹerbinotto means "dandy" or "fop." Most translations use the second meaning, but the original could be seen as a double-edged remark directed by Sparafucile at himself, commenting both on the duke's louche behavior and on his own subservient role as the pushover who has to wait on the dandy. —Trans.

12 "Come Verdi l'ha fatto," in *Tutte le cronache*, 2001.

13 The standard diapason, as is widely known, is set at 440 Hz.

14 *Carteggio Verdi-Ricordi* (Turin: EDT, 1994), 2: 423.

15 Verdi moved to Busseto from his birthplace in nearby Le Roncole, which has since been renamed Roncole Verdi.

16 "Maestro, se va avanti così rischiamo di fare un bel spettacolino."

17 "La bufera infernal, che mai non resta." Dante Alighieri, *Inferno*, V: 31.

18 In theatrical jargon, the fireproof metal barrier installed between the set and the audience.

19 The last episode of Stravinsky's *Rite of Spring*, in which the "chosen" adolescent dances to death, sacrificing herself to the gods.

20 "Splendido ragazzaccio dell'infuocato Sud, amico mio scanzonato e carissimo, fascinoso e irresistibile maestro."

21   When one addresses the queen of England, protocol actu-
     ally requires that the greeting begin with "Your Majesty" and
     then shift, over the course of the conversation, to "Ma'am."
     I found that funny—it's said not like "ham" but like "chum"
     or "farm"—because it sounds a lot like the accent people have
     in Molfetta. See *A–Z of Modern Manners* (London: Debrett's,
     2008), 157.

CHAPTER EIGHT

1   "Verimm' nu poco: 'a sinfonia 'e Bellini è na cusarella, e chella
    'lla ce 'a bevimme in nu mumento; 'o concerto 'e Ciaikoski è in
    repertorio, e pecciò co na prova mett'a posto 'sta robba. Doppo a
    chesto, Strauss: na prova, e vuie liggit' *Dall'Italia* coll'orchestra.
    Dint'a terzaa prova affermate 'a vuosta personalità, in tutto so'
    tre: maestro, avite na prova in cchiù."

2   "E cchi save 'o francese?"

3   "Ma quande mai a Surriento c'è stata 'a spiaggia?"

4   "'O maestro vo' 'e ccampane!"

5   "Sient' a me, ce sta na rammera llà ncoppa; vutt' abbascio 'a
    rammera."

CHAPTER NINE

1   The 1955 Danish film *Ordet* by Carl Theodor Dreyer appeared
    in English as *The Word*; here "the word" is extended to "the
    voice."—Trans.

2   Two Italian cyclists whose rivalry throughout the 1940s and
    1950s divided the country.—Trans.

3   The chapter of *Sono apparso alla Madonna* titled "Palco di prosa
    (Giuseppe Di Stefano)," in Carmelo Bene, *Opere* (Milan: Bom-
    piani, 1995), 1111–14.

4   See note 2, chapter 7.

5   Tobias Möller, "On the Reception of *Carmina Burana*," *Orff Today*, no. 9 (2006): 36.

CHAPTER TEN

1   Johann Wolfgang von Goethe, *Wilhelm Meisters Lehrjahre* (1795), published in English as *Wilhelm Meister's Apprenticeship*, trans. Thomas Carlyle (1874; New York: Limited Editions Club, 1959).—Trans.

2   In Ettore Petrolini's satire, first performed in Bologna in 1924, the eponymous Gastone sings, "I was born in a tux. When I was born, my mother didn't wrap me in swaddling clothes, no, she dolled me up in a little tux! I toddled around the house looking like a penguin."

3   "Eduardo," in *Opere*, 1146.

4   Marco Grondona, *La perfetta illusione: Ermione e l'opera seria rossiniana* (Lucca: Akademos & LIM, 1996).

CHAPTER ELEVEN

1   The soprano female lead of Verdi's opera set to the libretto by Temistocle Solera, in turn based on the tragedy *Attila, König der Hunnen* (Attila, King of the Huns) by Zacharias Werner. Odabella is orphaned when her father is killed, and avenges him by murdering Attila, the king who has fallen hopelessly (and unrequitedly) in love with her, during their wedding celebration.

2   Seneca, *Letters to Lucilius*, 1.12.1–4: "I do owe one thing to my villa: everywhere I look here my old age appears before me."

3   Di Giacomo, "A Capemonte," in *Poesie e Prose*, 38: "L'anne ca passano chi po' acchiappà?"

4   *Letţte Briefe aus Stalingrad*, published in English as *Last Letters from Stalingrad*, trans. Franz Schneider and Charles Gullans (New York: Morrow, 1962). This quote is from the third letter,

in which a pianist who has lost his fingers to frostbite is telling his girlfriend about listening to one of his fellow soldiers who was also a pianist, Kurt Hahnke, play in a side street just off Red Square, on a piano that had been pulled out of a house just before it blew up.

5   One of Italy's most notorious prisons, located in the Naples neighborhood of that name, known for detaining major convicts affiliated with organized crime.—Trans.

6   Dante Alighieri, *Purgatorio*, VII: 10–11, 18: "Qual è colui che cosa innanzi sé subita vede ond'e' si maraviglia" and "O pregio etterno del loco ond'io fui."

7   Many films have been made about Schubert, eight of them between 1933 and 1970 alone. I'm referring here to the 1954 film *Sinfonia d'amore* (*Symphony of Love*), directed by Glauco Pellegrini, with Claude Laydu, Marina Vlady, and Lucia Bosè. Four years later, in *Das Dreimäderlhaus* (*House of the Three Girls*) by Ernst Marischka, the lead was played by Karl Böhm's son, Karlheinz.

AFTERWORD

1   Symphony no. 9 in C Major, D. 944.—Trans.

2   The maestro's comment refers to the fifth sonata, "Sitio," bars 60ff.

3   Mozart, *Vesperae solennes de confessore*, K. 339, bars 54–58, "Dixit." (I reluctantly, and only so as not to come across as a snob, keep the blunder ["solennes"] that everyone, and I'm not sure why—as with Beethoven's *Missa* [*solemnis*]—always uses.)

4   See Richard Wagner, "Über das Dirigieren," in *Gesammelte Schriften und Dichtungen* (Leipzig: Fritzsch, 1898), 8: 268, "*herunter*blasen zu lassen"; 276, "eine fatale Vorliebe für das *Herunter*- oder *Vorüber*jagen"; 278, "wenn es ausdruckslos und matt *herunter*gespielt würde"; 279, "fast im Presto *herunter*ge-jagte"; 284, "die Maxime des flotten Darüber*hinweg*gehens." See

also Theodor W. Adorno, "Die Meisterschaft des Maestro," in *Gesammelte Schriften* (Frankfurt am Main: Suhrkamp, 1978), 16: 54ff.

5   The technical term *stringere* means "to condense" or "to tighten."—Trans.

6   The sensation that, even in the whirlwind of the Allegro vivace, it sped up even more was already present in measures 11.3, 5, etc., and then reached a climax at 11.17, 21, etc.

7   Said by Muti during the rehearsal of Giorgio's aria, "Del suo mal non v'affliggete," in *Nina, ossia La pazza per amore* by Giovanni Paisiello, at the lines "Ognun salta, ognun s'accende, chi dà baci, chi li rende." Regarding the ephemeral and therefore unequaled nature of theatrical representation—as usual—Fedele D'Amico said it best: "It is therefore nearly impossible that an opera, even under the same baton, will turn out the same in two different performances. . . . That is precisely why, thank God, theater is theater" ("Quando Lucia comincia a cantare," in *Tutte le cronache*, 34).

8   "Intervallo del cuore," as defined by Gino Stefani; see G. Stefani, L. Marconi, and F. Ferrari, *Gli intervalli musicali: Dall'esperienza alla teoria* (Milan: Bompiani, 1990), 9–24. The "minacce" theme begins with a sixth note, while the "destino" theme concludes on a sixth note.

9   Hugo Riemann, *System der musikalischen Rhythmik und Metrik* (Leipzig: Breitkopf & Härtel, 1903), 9; I have translated the German *mittleren Zeiten*, literally "average time," as "correct tempo."

10   Walther Dürr and Walter Gerstenberg, "Rhythmus, Metrum, Takt," in *Die Musik in Geschichte und Gegenwart* (first edition), 11: 385.

11   This observation was made by Karl-Ernst Behne, who continues, "Theories of that sort consequently affirm that there must be a relationship (up until now, truthfully, this has not been solidly proven) between the occasionally preferred tempos and some biological function. Yet the congruence between the average pulse and that of the most common metronomic rates neverthe-less remains incontestable. . . . And even those who, like Sachs,

do not believe at all in the relationship between tempo and pulse, still allow that there is such a thing as a normal tempo ("correct tempo")" ("Tempo, B. Systematisch," in *MGG¹*, first edition, 16: 1836).

12 The technical term *tempo primo* refers to an agogic accent in the score.—Trans.

13 Saint Paul: "The letter killeth, but the spirit giveth life" (2 Cor. 3:6).

14 Wagner, "Glucks Ouvertüre zu 'Iphigenia in Aulis,'" in *Gesammelte Schriften und Dichtungen*, 5: 117.

15 Ibid., 114.

16 Ibid., 115. The first two examples are from Bülow's piano reductions (1858, prepared for Wagner's reworking of Gluck's masterpiece and therefore rightly averse to any changes in tempo) and the Peters edition, no. 9752 (which accentuates the consideration paid in "Gluck's Ouvertüre," marking a *Grave* at bar 19, changing the tempo, but for the better!); however, one often finds an *Allegro* at bar 19 (see the last example, the duet piano reduction by Hugo Ulrich, written for "four hands"—that is, two pianists playing a duet on the same piano) which consecrates the erroneous practice common in the mid–nineteenth century: "the German editions of the overture, and, using those as a point of departure, perhaps the French ones as well, end up introducing, de facto, the inappropriate *Allegro*" (ibid., 114).

17 Everyone rushes it a little—in order: Gianandrea Gavazzeni, Georges Prêtre, Tullio Serafin.

18 In Parma, May 12, 1995, with the Orchestra Filarmonica della Scala.

19 See note 23.

20 At the Festival di Ravenna, with the band from Delianuova (near Reggio Calabria).

21 Emilio Tadini, "Benvenuti nella mia isola della solitudine," *Sette* (weekly supplement to *Corriere della Sera*), 1994, no. 48, p. 22; Enzo Biagi, "Un uomo 'semplice,'" *Amadeus* 3, no. 19 (1991): 32.

22 "Oggi Verdi è in gran forma," in *Tutte le cronache*, 851.

23 "Harmonically speaking the two themes fit where they touch,

and awkwardly even then." Julian Budden, *The Operas of Verdi*, rev. ed. (Oxford: Clarendon: 1991), 2: 446.

24 This musical indication [using the antiquated *nudrita* for *nutrita* and literally meaning "with a well-fed voice"—Trans.] appears in the manuscript score. I spoke with Fabrizio Della Seta about this passage, once again admiring his skill and grace. Note, however, that the manuscript score also has a part just below the first flute played by the second flute, not the piccolo. For similar restraint, averse to the dominance of the higher voice—in a passage from the last movement of Mozart's [*Prussian*] Quartet, K. 575—see the splendid interview of Rudolf Kolisch, *Zur Theorie der Aufführung: Ein Gespräch mit Berthold Türcke*: "T.: In this passage I hear the lower part much more clearly than the higher part. / K.: It is quite likely that the second violin is stronger, more sonorous. In any case, I made a concerted effort to avoid the opposite situation: that soprano sound! That is how I hear it, with the higher voice more restrained— / T.: —to provide the harmony. / K.: Precisely!" (*Musik-Konzepte* 29–30 (January 1983), 77.

25 These are the remarkable words the composer Hans Werner Henze used to describe the ideal sound for his *König Hirsch* or *Re Cervo* (The Stag King) and other Italian-influenced operas in *Essays* (Mainz: Schott, 1964), 29.

26 Bene, *Opere*, 1017.

27 Wagner, *Über das Dirigieren*, 268ff.

28 He refers to the first violins' part in bars 119–22 of "Sitio."

29 The flute part at bars 90–94 of "Consummatum est."

30 Regarding Wagner's text and the fashion of using grace notes, see my book *Il compito del traduttore: «Ave verum corpus» e la fortuna di Mozart* (Pisa: SEU, 2006), 26–43. See also, particularly with regard to the Schröder-Devrient episode, *Il compito del traduttore*, vol. 2, *Wagner «de optimo genere interpretandi»* (Pisa: SEU, 2008), 81–91.

31 Mozart, *Vesperae*, "Confitebor," bars 66–69.

32 This refers to bars 326–43 in the prologue of the *Götterdämmerung*, just before sunrise.

33 Vartan's version of the song, titled "Caro Mozart," is from 1971, and instead of simply turning one's nose up, it is worth noting that the French pop singer chose to use Italian lyrics.

34 Gino Stefani, *Capire la musica* (Rome: Espresso strumenti, 1978), 66.

35 "Die jungen Dirigieren" (1896), in *Heinrich Schenker als Essayist und Kritiker*, ed. Hellmut Federhofer (Hildesheim: Olms, 1990), 175–81.

36 "Dixit," bars 117–22.

37 Wagner, *Über das Dirigieren*, 283. In order to understand how essential he considered it, note how many times the concept reappeared: pp. 269, 272, 279, 282ff., 286ff., and 295.

38 Socrates's final words are in Plato, *Phaedo*, 118, and Nietzsche's gloss appears in *Der sterbende Sokrates*, no. 340 in *Die fröhliche Wissenschaft*, IV: "Whether it was death, or the poison, or piety, or wickedness—something or other loosened his tongue at that moment, and he said: 'O Crito, I owe a cock to Asclepius.' For him who has ears, this ludicrous and terrible 'last word' implies: 'O Crito, *life is a long sickness!*' Is it possible! A man like him, who had lived cheerfully and to all appearance as a soldier—was a pessimist! He had merely put on a good demeanor towards life, and had all along concealed his ultimate judgment, his profoundest sentiment!" These lines are an ideal commentary to the conclusion of Rossini's opera.

39 The technical term *basso di lamento*, literally a "bass of lament," is also known as a Phrygian tetrachord.—Trans.

40 Schumann, *Fantasiestücke*, op. 12, I.3, "Warum?" in the last twelve bars.

41 The well-known piece that Luigi Boccherini rewrote several times with slight variations. Only the modern instrumentation by Luciano Berio—*Quattro versioni originali della Ritirata notturna di Madrid di L. Boccherini sovrapposte e trascritte per orchestra* (1975)—has managed to capture its "content drawn from real life," simulating a local band that approaches the audience along a road, reaching a roaring sound, and then continues onward, fading to the point where it is barely audible. This effect, which

is intensely felt onstage in many operas (to note just a few of
the more obvious examples: *La Damnation de Faust*, III, "La
retraite"; *La Bohème*, II, no. 27, Allegro alla marcia; *Tannhäuser*,
prelude, bars 1–80, and scenes I.3a and III.1a), almost always
runs the risk, as sometimes happens with Rossini's crescendos,
of getting lost amid orchestras' poor dynamic conduct—as also
happens, for example, in Mozart's *Marriage of Figaro*.

42   Jean Victor Hocquard, *Le nozze di Figaro di Mozart* (Milan:
     Emme, 1981), 129.

43   Massimo Mila, *Lettura delle «Nozze di Figaro»* (Turin: Einaudi,
     1979), 143.

44   Thereby instinctively realizing the desire of the best Mozartian
     theatrical historian, Stefan Kunze: "aber auch gehört das ganze
     Finale in die Kategorie der szenischen Musik; dies bedeutet,
     das alle Stücke ausdrücklich als reale Musik, wenngleich nicht
     als Bühnen Musik" (the entire finale belongs to the category of
     scenic music; this means that it is to be understood as real music,
     even without strictly being "stage music"), in *Mozarts Opern*
     (Stuttgart: Reclam, 1984), 259.

45   In this wonderful text Paul Bekker points out how the "sym-
     phonic" effect is among the best possibilities for a crescendo and
     the inevitable decrescendo: "The illustration . . . of an approach-
     ing and then receding crowd . . . was a welcome opportunity for
     the use of crescendo and decrescendo," such that "every episode
     on the stage justified an expansion of orchestral expression" (*The
     Story of the Orchestra* [New York: Norton, 1936], 76, 75).

46   "Fragment über Musik und Sprache," in *Gesammelte Schriften*,
     16: 253; translation by Rodney Livingstone in *Quasi una
     Fantasia: Essays on Modern Music* (London: Verso, 1998), 3–4.

47   Keeps himself at a distance from the execution.

48   The original uses the term *battitore libero*, literally "free beater"
     and by extension "free kicker," a defensive position in soccer that
     refers to a defender who is freed of the responsabilty of mark-
     ing duties; therefore, this is an ironic play on words referring to
     conductors who slavishly keep the beat and do little else—a type
     of conductor also referred to as a *battisolfa*, literally "one who

beats sol-fa," someone who keeps time in solfeggio. The humorous irony of his wordplay between sports and music is lost in translation.—Trans.

49 Adriano Lualdi, *L'arte di dirigere l'orchestra* (Milan: Hoepli, 1940), 55. These were, more or less, the words Romano Gandolfi uttered after a performance of *Nabucco* wherein pathos reigned supreme from the first note to the last. Gandolfi had had music in his blood ever since, as a child, he played the accordion in the local dance halls around Fidenza, and as an adult he understood Adorno's idea of "copying" or "transcribing" better than anyone else. He once addressed a girl who had complimented him with an absolute bashfulness and highly noble reserve: "Ma'am, sometimes I sensed that they wanted to 'go,' and so I let them go" (Busseto, July 27, 2001).

50 Constantin Stanislavski, *An Actor Prepares*, trans. Elizabeth Reynolds Hapgood (New York: Theatre Arts, 1936), 37. He had invited the student to act out the following scene: the very day her mother has been fired, a girl loses the precious brooch that a friend gave her to help out.

51 *Ave verum corpus*, K. 618. What Muti captured is mentioned throughout texts on Mozart: Mila, *Lettura*, 176ff. ("sudden solemnity, *sancta sanctorum*, the prayer becomes beseeching, more intense, grace descends from above, a religious ambience, a religious chorale"), and Hocquard, *Le nozze*, 163 ("its spirit is close to that of the last attack, on the words 'in mortis,' of the motet").

52 The author uses the Latin phrase *inclinans se deorsum* to describe when Muti "stoops down."—Trans.

53 These lines are from the magnificent and often overlooked Lualdi, *L'arte*, 54; italics mine.

54 It cannot be repeated enough that, every time a piece was played in two places, the better one, alas, was almost never the one performed at La Scala, because the more "human-scale" halls of the theaters in smaller towns gave them an invaluable advantage.

55 "Cors de chasse," in *Selected Writings of Guillaume Apollinaire*, ed. Roger Shattuck (New York: New Directions, 1971), 131.

Readers who wish to know more about hunting horns can consult the curious book *Nove arabeschi e un "Messaggio" di romantico affetto al "corno da caccia" passato dal bosco all'orchestra* by Arnaldo Ferriguto (Verona: Chiamenti, 1952).

56   This remarkable quote is from *Sono apparso alla Madonna*, in *Opere*, 1074.

57   *Opere*, 1010.

58   The passage in question was Giorgio's aria, "Del suo mal non v'affliggete," from *Nina*, act 1, scene 4, at the second verse, "Se vedeste, mio signore."

59   Carl Schroeder, *Katechismus des Dirigierens und Taktierens* (Leipzig: Hesse, 1889), 37.

60   S. D'Amico's entry for "Dramma" in the *Enciclopedia italiana* (1949), 13: 202.

61   Antonin Artaud, "La mise en scène et la métaphysique" (1932), in *Le Théâtre et son double*, in *Oeuvres complètes* (Paris: Gallimard, 1964), 4: 39–42; translation by Mary Caroline Richards in *The Theater and Its Double* (New York: Grove, 1958), 33.

62   Bene, "Marlowe," in *Opere*, 1017.

63   For such a reading see, on *noema*, Clemens Kühn, *Analyse lernen* (Kassel: Bärenreiter, 1994), 68.

64   Partially in dialect: "Queste sono formule! Jamme!! Non è Beethoven!!!"

65   Hans Christian Andersen, "The Story of a Mother," in *The Complete Andersen*, trans. Jean Hersholt, 6 vols. (New York: Limited Editions Club, 1949).

66   "And so music is, I would almost say, the moral atmosphere that fills up the place in which the characters of the drama carry out the performance." Transcribed by Antonio Zanolini in *Una passeggiata in compagnia di Rossini*, reprinted in Luigi Rognoni, *Gioacchino Rossini* (Turin: Einaudi, 1977), 379.

67   "I say that the stage is a concrete physical place which asks to be filled, to be given its own concrete language to speak" (Artaud, "Mise en scène," 45; trans. Richards, 37).

68   The musical episode referred to is from *I puritani*, I, no. 9, bars

12–29, and the figure evidently uses one of the sketches Luigi
Nono made for *Verso Prometeo*. See Hans Peter Haller, "La
tecnica del 'live electronic' allo Studio sperimentale di Friburgo,"
in *Luigi Nono e il suono elettronico* (Milan: Milano Musica, 2000),
213–17.

69 Elias Canetti, "Aspekte der Macht: Der Dirigent," in *Masse und
Macht* (Munich: Hanser, 1960), 468–70.

70 Adorno, "Die Meisterschaft," 55.

71 Paul Hindemith, "Interpreten," in *Komponist in seiner Welt*
(Zürich: Atlantis, 1994), 171ff.; it is clear that his aversion to the
conductor is essentially authoritarian, and it betrays—as does
that of his aforementioned fellow countrymen—the frightening,
obscene memory of the Führer.

72 Pinzauti, "Entusiasmo di altri tempi per I puritani al Comunale,"
La Nazione, December 2, 1970, reprinted in *Riccardo Muti al
Teatro Comunale*, 17. Muti had already conducted a few other
pieces at the Teatro Comunale, but it was that evening that he
first established an unexpected, sudden rapport with the audience, and the illustrious critic recognized that with his typical
objective honesty.

73 The reference here is to Fabrizio De André's 1973 song "Il bombarolo," in which a clerical worker plans to bomb a parliament
building but misses, blowing up a newsstand instead and finding
his girlfriend's picture on every front page (as if he could see
into the future).—Trans.

74 This definition is from Niccolò Tommaseo's *Dizionario*, the most
important dictionary of the Italian language produced during
national unification; I do not know how many of us feel this way,
but I am in the good company of Fedele D'Amico: "'We here in
England consider Giulini the best conductor Italy has produced
since Toscanini.' I wholeheartedly agreed." ("Insuperabile
sarà lei!" in *Tutte le cronache*, 1613); "Giulini is the opposite:
the sound, dynamics, etc., are all born of the phrasing; and his
phrasing is more intimate, more personal than it is conspicuous,
but it is highly penetrating and all-powerful" ("Stasera dirige

Dominiddio," ibid., 1655); refusing the albums of his adored
Furtwängler: "you can keep your albums, I would rather refresh
my memory with his reincarnations, so I prefer to go hear
Giulini" (ibid., 1505ff.).

75 Artaud, "Première lettre sur le langage," in *Le théâtre*, 127; trans.
Richards, *Theater and Its Double*, 106.

76 "Palco di prosa (Giuseppe di Stefano)," in *Opere*, 1112.

77 Ibid., 997.

78 Ibid., 1006.

79 Bene attributes these words to Verdi; see *Opere*, 1011.

80 Artaud, "Mise en scène," 40; trans. Richards, 33. He goes on to
write of "Le grésillement d'un feu d'artifice à travers le bombar-
dement nocturne des étoiles."

81 *Nabucco*, symphony, bars 207ff.; *Nina*, beginning of act 1 (which
the maestro refers to); *Figaro*, overture, bars 61ff.

82 Bene, *Opere*, 1011ff. and 1005.

83 This is the terminology with which the first Latin translations
of Aristotle by Valla (1498) and Pazzi (1536) rendered the Greek
word *òpsis*. Bene's readers will not be surprised by the fact that
the second term became "from that moment on the term generally used in commentary on the *Poetics* edited in Latin"; see
Francesco Donadi's essay "Per una interpretazione aristotelica
del dramma," in *Poetica e stile* (Padua: Liviana, 1976), 6.

84 Number 3,118 of Nietzsche's *Posthumous Notes*.

85 Riccardo Muti to the inmates of Bollate prison the evening of
January 18, 2010.

Index of Names

Abbado, Claudio, 92
Abert, Hermann, 184
Adorno, Theodor W., 152, 166, 182–83, 198, 200, 225n49
Agrippa, Menenius, 22
Ajello, Ugo, 22–23, 28
Alagna, Roberto, 98
Albergati, Francesco, 213n11
Alberti, Luciano, 41, 61
Albertini, Gabriele, 116, 123
Alfano, Franco, 86
Alighieri, Dante, 12, 118, 162, 210n12, 216n17, 219n6
Altobelli, Salvatore, 24
Andersen, Hans Christian, 197
Apollinaire, Guillaume, 189
Archipova, Irina, 65
Aristotle, 196, 199, 204, 207, 228n83
Arrau, Claudio, 141
Arruga, Lorenzo, 32
Artaud, Antonin, 165, 194, 197, 201–2, 203, 205, 207, 226n67, 228n80
Audi, Pierre, 68

Bach, Johann Sebastian, 23, 46, 48, 49, 213n8
Badini, Carlo Maria, 95
Balducci (cellist), 47–48
Barbieri-Nini, Marianna, 58